Don't Make a
Black Woman Take Off
Her Earrings

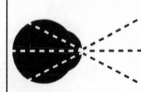

This Large Print Book carries the
Seal of Approval of N.A.V.H.

DON'T MAKE A BLACK WOMAN TAKE OFF HER EARRINGS

MADEA'S UNINHIBITED COMMENTARIES ON LOVE AND LIFE

TYLER PERRY

THORNDIKE PRESS

An imprint of Thomson Gale, a part of The Thomson Corporation

Detroit • New York • San Francisco • New Haven, Conn. • Waterville, Maine • London

THOMSON

GALE

While the author has made every effort to provide accurate telephone numbers and Internet addresses at the time of publication, neither the publisher nor the author assumes any responsibility for errors, or for changes that occur after publication. Further, the publisher does not have any control over and does not assume any responsibility for author or third-party websites or their content.

Thorndike Press® Large Print African-American.

The text of this Large Print edition is unabridged.

Other aspects of the book may vary from the original edition.

Set in 16 pt. Plantin.

LIBRARY OF CONGRESS CATALOGING-IN-PUBLICATION DATA

Perry, Tyler.
  Don't make a black woman take off her earrings : Madea's uninhibited commentaries on love and life / by Tyler Perry.
    p. cm. — (Thorndike Press large print African-American)
  ISBN 0-7862-9107-9 (lg. print : alk. paper)
  1. Conduct of life — Fiction. 2. Large type books. I. Title. II. Title: Do not make a black woman take off her earrings.
  PS3616.E795D66 2006b
  813'.6 — dc22
                                                                    2006025559

U.S. Hardcover:
ISBN 13: 978-0-7862-9107-6
ISBN 10: 0-7862-9107-9

Published in 2006 by arrangement with Riverhead Books,
a division of Penguin Group (USA) Inc.

Printed in the United States of America on permanent paper
10 9 8 7 6 5 4 3 2 1

CONTENTS

FOREWORD

by Tyler Perry

Whoever came up with the saying that "it takes a village to raise a child" must have been thinking of my friend Madea. In the black community, Madea was the head of that village. Her name is the southern term for "mother dear." Madea used to be on every corner in every neighborhood when I was growing up and generations before. She used to be everywhere, but today she is missed. Back around the 1970s, the Madeas in our neighborhoods began to disappear and they have left an unmistakable void.

Everybody wants this kind of grandmother around. No matter what race you are, everybody wants to have a Madea in their family. She's not politically correct. She doesn't care about anything but what is honest and true. And she is always saying the least expected things. The other day, I asked Madea how she was feeling. She said, "I woke up this morning with a little numbness on the side of my hip. But it's all gone now. I just realized that I had slept on my vibrator."

People are so endeared to her because of her honesty. That's why I think she is so beloved. Some people have even told me they think we'd be better off if Madea were president of the United States. If that were the case, the country would be bankrupt, because she would spend all the money. I don't think the majority of the elite would approve of her policies. But the people would appreciate her as president. I think she would be as popular as President Clinton.

In the Madea administration, there would be no complicated international entanglements. There would be little if any talking with people of other cultures and other countries. If she doesn't speak the language, she's not one to sit there and wait for a translation. Madea's foreign policy would be "There ain't none." But we wouldn't have terrorists, either, because she would deal with them personally, from the bottom of her purse.

I think Madea has an opportunity to say everything that I can't say because, number one, I'm a man, and women get away with saying things a lot more than a man would. In our society, women are given much more latitude than men to have emotions and to express them. And, number two, she has been around for more than a few decades, so she can get away with stating some opinions I'd be afraid to say. And, number three, she just has a way of putting things — sometimes I'll have something I really want to say and then I'll just hear it coming out of Madea's mouth, in her own words.

In the beginning, I was really shocked about the things she said, the way she said them, and how she got away with it. But today I'm pretty shockproof with regard to Madea. Whatever comes up comes out. You just have to be ready for it. Madea and I have different, *extremely* different, ideas about life, raising children, diet — the list goes on. But there is a line that we walk together: we are both very loving and caring people.

I remember a guy on the corner of my neighborhood who wanted to be a Madea. He would come out of his house every morning with the curlers in his hair and a bandanna and just look around and see what the kids were doing. He would then run and tell their parents. But he was kind of illegitimate.

Looking at the authentic ones (my mother and aunt included), these women were not *trying* to be this Madea person. The responsibility of the neighborhood simply fell upon them. If somebody's child was doing something wrong, Madea got to them and straightened them out or she would go directly to the parents, and the parents straightened the kids out.

With parents, caregivers, and Madea there to keep an eye out, it was easier to give kids a chance to spread their wings. We have to allow our children to make mistakes and not shelter them too much, which is hard to do. The key is finding the balance between allowing them to hit the wall and bump their head, and protecting them from things that are extremely dangerous — that can destroy them and take their lives.

Because there are so few Madeas, children are pretty much raising themselves. So many parents have to work hard just to make ends meet. Madea used to watch out for these children.

My friend Madea has "attitude" that comes with wisdom. Back in our teens and twenties, we thought we knew everything and made all those foolish mistakes. Then, when we got a little older, at thirty, we started getting these flashes of light, revelations of what a great and lucky thing it was that we didn't get caught doing those stupid things back then. Around forty, if we're lucky, we stop lying to ourselves. Fifty and above, we've run out of patience for foolishness. Take me to the bottom line. When we get even older, it becomes more urgent. "I don't have that much time, I'm trying to enjoy my life, get away from me with your foolishness." That's pretty much Madea's thoughts and way of life.

I want to dedicate the spirit and intent of this book to all the Madeas and the mothers that I grew up with — to my mother, Maxine; my aunt, Mayola; Big Mabel Murphy; Viola; Olabea; Sylvia — all those women who were on the block on that one stretch down in New Orleans.

As you read on, I hope that you will enjoy your time together with Madea and have some good laughs. For those of you who are new to Madea and haven't seen her on the stage, on DVDs, or in film, I hope you can separate her great wisdom from some of the totally ridiculous things she sometimes has to say. You never know what she's going to say or do. She always keeps me on my guard!

INTRODUCTION

by "Madea" Mabel Simmons

The reason why I am writing this book is because I have lived a long life. It's been great. I've seen a lot of things. Every time I'm out in front of people, they ask me for advice. "Madea, what should I do about this? Madea, what should I do about that?" I tell people I've got problems of my own, but for some reason, they keep asking and they seem to like to listen to the advice that I've got to give. So, rather than writing a book about advice, I just want to talk. Maybe some of this stuff you can relate to, maybe not. Maybe some of it you can understand, maybe some of it you don't. If you are not a black person and you don't understand something, read that part to a friend who's black and ask for an explanation. If you don't have any black friends, make one on the bus. If they see you reading this book with my face on the cover, they will want to stop and talk to you.

13

This book is to help you understand that life is sometimes hard, and you have to laugh your way through it.

But first, I want to clear up one very important matter. I received no help at all from Mr. Tyler Perry in writing this book. He had absolutely nothing to do with it. These are not his opinions. The lawyers told me to tell you that. These opinions have only to do with Madea. Tyler Perry has nothing to do with Madea. We are two very separated individuals, okay! I don't know him that well. He don't know me that well. So this book is about Madea.

I met Tyler Perry when he was a little boy. I knew his mother and his auntie. They were all worried about him because he talked to himself. He walked around a lot by himself and spent a lot of time alone. We were really worried one day. We saw him with a pink dress on. He said it was because it was Mardi Gras, but I don't know. We were all very concerned.

To write this book, I sat down and recorded all of this on an old eight-track player I had in the closet and had it transcomposed by my friend Joel Brokaw. Everybody needs a friend like Joel. He's got hair like Gene Wilder and a heart like Oprah.

I decided to write all this stuff down because I'm so tired of saying the same advice over and over again. So if anybody asks me from now on, I can just pick up the book and say, "Did you read this? Unless you read the book, don't ask me no questions." That's what Jesus is telling people these days. I believe he's saying to them, "If you have not read the Book, don't ask me no questions." So read the book. This is your official guide to all things Madea.

Consider this book your one big fortune cookie. Every page that you turn to will be a new fortune. Now, if you're looking for the cookies — I ate them. So take it as you will.

■ ■ ■ ■

PART ONE
THE MAKING OF MADEA

■ ■ ■ ■

People often say that the truth hurts. Hell no, it hurts even more if you do a whole bunch of foolishness to try to avoid it. So, now you've been warned for what's to follow!

Skeletons in the Closet

Everybody's got skeletons in the closet. Every once in a while, you've got to open up the closet and let the skeletons breathe. Half the time, the very thing you think that's going to destroy you or ruin you is the very thing that nobody cares about. My advice to anybody with skeletons is dust them off every now and then — as long as your closet ain't full of them. It's not good to have more than two or three.

What I have learned in this life is that you can never be ashamed of where you come from. So as you read some of this stuff, especially when I'm talking about my family and folks, keep in mind that I'm going to keep it real. Some people think that keeping it real will get you in trouble, but I'm going to tell it like it is.

The first memory from my childhood is so beautiful. It was lovely. I was looking out of the window. It was autumn. The leaves were changing, everything was golden brown, and the wind was blowing. The sky was blue with white clouds passing slowly. At that moment, I was sitting there thinking, Wow, I am so very, very blessed to be on this earth. Just as I was getting ready to raise my hands and say, "Thank you, Jesus," my momma slapped the hell out of me on the back of my head and said, "You ain't finished washing them dishes yet! Stop staring out that window and finish the dishes!" So that's my earliest remembrance. I must have been about five.

We started cleaning the house at three. In that day, we didn't have no remote controls and vacuum cleaners. If you wanted all of that stuff, you had children. That's what they were for. So that was my job: I was the automatic dishwasher. My brother was the lawn mower. I had another sister who was the remote control — every time they wanted to change the channel on the TV. Every time the family wanted a new technology, it was called children.

I grew up in a little house on a hill in the country in a little town named Greensburg, Louisiana. Maybe it was more like a shack. We had to stuff newspapers into the walls because we didn't have insulation back then. But it was nice. We had an outhouse. We didn't have much, but we had love.

And I had many, many, many uncles. Every time my daddy went to work, one of my uncles would come over. So there were plenty of family members always around. Most of the uncles' names were Johnson for some reason: Uncle Little Johnson, Uncle Big Johnson, Uncle Wide Johnson, Uncle Crooked Johnson — everybody's name was always Johnson. I could never figure that out.

Britney Spears grew up in the same area. She, of course, came many years later. It was a little different today than when I grew up there. Now they have trailers. As I said, I grew up in a shack, she grew up in a trailer, but we are all in the same park, not too far from each other. I knew her great-grandmother. What was her name? Litany Spears? That's right, Litany. Yeah, I didn't like her, and she didn't like me.

It was a small house. We had a living room, a kitchen, the outhouse, and one bedroom. All of us there in the one room. But you know, it was all good. There was a foot tub that we would all take baths in. We'd have to get the water from the well and warm it up. You had to stay clean when you live in such close quarters. If you smelled bad, my mother would be the first one to knock you on the side of head and tell you to take a bath. There were two beds: one for my momma and daddy, and the other for all us children — that was another good reason to smell good, sleeping in the same bed.

My daddy was the nicest man you'd never want to meet — but not too bright, though. Looking back, I realize just how dumb he was when I remember him coming home once and finding one of the uncles there. My momma introduced him as Uncle Lowdown. My father shook his hand and invited him to stay for dinner. You see, my daddy had an accident. He worked at the sawmill and one of the logs fell down and hit him upside his head. That side of his brain was never too together after that, but he was a good provider.

Of course, growing up like that, all together with seven or eight people, you have to stand up for yourself. I had to fight all the time. That might have something to do with who I am now.

THE ORIGINAL MADEA

My mother was feisty and stern. She *was* the original Madea. I'm Madea Lite compared to her. That woman was Madea Over the Top. She was a cusser. She didn't have little guns. She had shotguns and razors. People would come by the house for protection. She was there with Harriet Tubman — they were friends, my momma and Harriet Tubman. They played cards together. Yeah, I know what you're thinking. She was quite old. People don't live that long no more. This has a simple explanation: Harriet Tubman ate nothing but wheatgrass. It was all they had. So they stayed healthy. My momma also was friends with Mary McLeod Bethune-Cookman. My momma was a civil rights activator. She activated in the civil rights. The only one she could never have worked with was Dr. King. They wouldn't have let her in the marches because she was too violent. So you might say I picked up a few traits from her.

My momma was a big woman, too. I'm small compared to her. They called her Big Mabel Murphy. She would have been the entire W of the WNBA. It would have been the WWNBA, the Wide Women's National Basketball Association.

My mother was never a praying woman. She was a cussing Christian. She would go to church on Sunday and then cuss everybody out the remaining days of the week. I remember how she had her hands full with my brother. He would always be in trouble. My father was getting senile and could never do anything with him. Every time my brother Frederick would be in trouble — and he would always get into all kinds of trouble, especially when he was older — my mother would go and bail him out. Then, one day, she changed. She got the call but just turned over and went back to sleep.

Don't get me wrong, my mother was very gentle and mild-mannered, a very kind and peaceful woman . . . until you got her started. Now, what, you may ask, could get her started? If the wind blew the wrong way, that would get her started. We didn't have a car, but if the mule didn't get hitched up fast enough, she would get started. If the dust blew into the house after she had cleaned, all hell would break loose. The common house-fly? She would start shooting. We would all know to duck until she got that fly. But back in the day, you wouldn't dare tell her she was crazy. She needed what we call today Xanax.

Our neighbors didn't live so close. That's why my voice is so strong. I could holler all the way across the fields. That's the way we talked back then. We didn't have no cell phones. We would go out on the porch and yell. If you came home after a date one night and you wanted to talk to that person later on, you had to holler all your business. "Was it good? Did you enjoy yourself?" That would set my mother off, too. She'd go and beat the hell out of us.

Out in the country, we had chickens, cows, pigs, horses . . . No, we didn't have horses. We had mules that we wanted to be horses because we couldn't afford real ones. I worked in the fields planting beans and corn, but I wouldn't pick no cotton. I won't even open a bottle of aspirin because I don't want to touch that ball of cotton.

I must have been about sixteen when we moved to the city. My daddy started getting Social Security, and my momma decided that she wanted to move up. So we moved down to New Orleans into a shotgun house. It was beautiful. She fit right in. Big Mabel Murphy fit right in down there on Bourbon Street. I soon realized that all my uncles were down there, too. They would always hang out at this place they called a Hop House. She would go down there to hop around. At least that's how I understood it then.

Growing up, I didn't feel shamed about my momma, but I was a little bit embarrassed about all my uncles. You are who you are and growing up where you are for a reason. Because I was raised around all of the foolishness, I guess I just accepted it. Maybe that's why I had no problem being a stripper. You know, my stage name was Delicious. I invented "drop it like it's hot." Now, I have to "let it down like it's warm." But the way I grew up, I realized that I didn't want my daughter to have all those uncles. So once Cora was born — and that wasn't too long after we moved to the city — I decided I was going to have only one child, and I was going to limit myself to one uncle per year.

BECOMING MADEA

People ask, how did I get started being known as Madea instead of just plain Mabel Simmons? That's my real name. I didn't really find myself until after my mother got sick and all the uncles stopped coming around and she really needed me. She told me a lot of things about life. I've tried to remember all of it and take it with me. She told me a lot about taking care of yourself. "There ain't no man going to do something for you that you can't do for yourself. Get out there and make it happen for yourself." My mother was strong, too strong. She was six foot eight and weighed 410 pounds. She was almost as big as Paul Bunyan and his blue ox, Babe.

Every Madea gets her values and spirit from her mother. It was passed down. I thank God I had a good, strong one. It's a lintiage that is passed down. You get the good things or you get the bad things. I just tried to take it all. This temper comes from my momma. The good, gentle side comes from her, too. But the one that don't take no stuff is one of those personalities that she had. I could swear she was letsophrenic. Letsophrenic — it's a disorder where people are crazy and hear a bunch of voices and let so many people talk to them — that's letsophrenic.

I'm not quite as harsh as my mother was. I give people the benefit of the doubt, mostly just because it's a different day and time. See, back then, you ain't had nothing, and when they came up to you, you know what they wanted from you. But nowadays, you never know what people want because there's so much craziness and foolishness going on. So I try to give them a little more lead way. But they ain't going to sucker me. I ain't nobody's sucker.

When did I know that I was a Madea? I must have been about thirty, because Cora was a big girl when this happened. There was this one girl in the neighborhood, she was having trouble with her husband. I went over there and beat the hell out of him. He was a pretty big man, and I surprised myself with my own strength. Now, I've always been a big woman — not fat as hell, like this, but big. But that day I learned that I have more than the strength of a man. And that girl, she said to me, "Get the hell out of my house! I don't want you hurting him!"

I realized maybe I needed to keep my damned mouth shut and keep to my own business. I also learned that the power of helping people is wonderful but not always appreciated. So that was the moment I realized that Madea was something special and that I shouldn't waste my superpowers. I found out that when I and my big old 68 DX that's on my chest enter the room, we can make a difference. Wonder twins activate.

Now, up to this time, before I was thirty, I was preoccupied raising Cora and working. I worked as a stripper for as long as I could, from my late teens up to my early twenties. Something happened by the time I was twenty-five or twenty-six. I don't know why it's so, but the pounds start coming. They decide that they are going to go where the hell they want to go, and you can't tell them what to do. Then I realized what the Bible said about "from this earth you came, to this dirt you shall return." So as you look at your body when it's getting older, everything starts going back toward the dirt. That's what was happening to me; I realized I was going to hit the dirt at some point. (Men have that problem, too. When everything starts hitting the dirt, they can't get it up! When they get older, it points down to the dirt. Some people take a longer time to get back to the dirt because they ain't start with much. But some people get there a little sooner.) Anyway, even though I was young, I still had to do something besides stripping.

After the baby and all that other stuff, things aren't tight and firm no more. My tips went from two or three hundred dollars a night down to seven. I knew I had to get another job. I tried to go into the workforce, but it's hard for someone with my personality to work in corporate America. I worked for a big company that made paper toilet seat-protector covers. It's a noble cause and all, but I just couldn't bring myself to care very much about it. So that didn't last long. I couldn't get along with the people in the corporate office. They wanted me to work harder, and the amount of money they was paying me, I said I needed to find something else to do.

I knew waiting around for child support was a big waste of time, and I wasn't going to be on welfare. My mother would have turned over in both of her graves if she had known I was ever on welfare. (She was a big woman, so they had to cut her in half and bury her in two places.)

Now, I had my house. I believe in ownership. I bought a house and a car when I was stripping, and I was saving to get money to send Cora to college and give her everything that she needed.

Then I discovered the business of husbands. That's how I made my money from that point on. Insurance. Praise God for insurance. And so my days were spent watching soap operas — we called them "the stories" — especially *The Young and the Restless.* By the time the first one came on, Cora would be out of the house, on her way to school. I'd just sit there smoking and eating. Then I got up and did some exercising. Going from the bed to the kitchen and back into the bed would be one exercise. I'd wait a little while, clean up a little. I might make up the bed if it was a good day. Or I'd wait for Cora to come home and do everything. When you have kids, it's like early retirement. After they come home from school, you get them to do every damned thing and you just sit around doing whatever you want to do.

But it turned out that this kind of early retirement wasn't for me, sitting around cooped up all day, avoiding the neighbors —

Brown on one side and on the other, Inez.

I became a Black Pantheress. I was what you'd call a "natural woman" — in other words, I had an Afro like Angela Davis. I had the Afro, the bell bottoms, and the high platform shoes. All that stuff that's back in style now. I didn't start to get a perm until the late '80s when the Jheri curls came out. I've always been a little behind the times. I wore my Afro when it wasn't the style no more. I was "power to the people." The Black Pantheresses were the ones from the South who couldn't afford to come up to the North, where the real ones were. The way we looked, we were more like Black Pandas, but we called ourselves Pantheresses.

We tried to change society. I'm glad Rosa stayed on that bus, because if it had been me, I would have been dead, because I would have been fighting. You know, she was a woman who had class and grace. She could sit there and deal with it. But I would have punched that bus driver in the face and been waiting for Bull Connor and all them to bring all the dogs in Birmingham to come get me.

I tried to do some of the sit-ins. I wanted to go to the March on Washington with all those people. But I got a letter from them saying, DO NOT COME ANYWHERE NEAR US

BECAUSE WE HAVE HEARD ABOUT YOUR HISTORY. When you work on the pole and you carry a pistol, all the dignitaries don't want to be around you for some reason.

I didn't care. I did my own march. We did a march on Baronne Street. That's a street in New Orleans where we marched up the block. We got a whole bunch. It was twenty-two people. But all of us were as fat as hell, so we marched a good fifteen feet and everybody went to Burger King. They wanted us to do that boycott, too, like Rosa, where nobody would ride the bus. I said, Hell no, I'm going to get on this bus. Let them do that in Montgomery, 'cause they're smaller there. I was too big to be walking all that around.

Those times have come and gone. There are so many things going wrong these days, it calls for straight talk. So, again, I hope you don't mind that I'm going to tell it like it is.

Remember, I am the fourth generation of strippers. My mother was a stripper and a part-time prostitute. She did what she had to do to get the bills paid, and it was passed on to me. People call that a "generational curse," but I've broken that with my daughter, Cora. She was so embarrassed when I came to school to get her in my ho shorts and big platform boots. I don't know why it bothered her. She's so saved, she don't even take off her clothes in front of the mirror. She thinks if she sees herself, it's a sin. Maybe I went too far with her. She became so religious that she listens to the Bible on tape in her sleep. Everybody's too worried about being "right," about "fitting in." I am a size twenty-nine. I'm six foot five and two hundred and something . . . something pounds . . . okay, three hundred. So, I can't blend in. I can't begin to blend in. I've never in my life blended in. So, I'm not going to start now. If you like me, fine. If you don't like me, even better. You've already bought the book.

Something else I hope this book will do is to help people understand that you have to feel good about yourselves. It doesn't matter what other people say. You don't have to go keeping up with the Joneses. Hell, I ain't known anybody named Jones in my neighborhood.

The grass is always greener on the other side, but the water bill is higher. Teach a man how to fish, and the man who sells boats will be happy. I can't give you all of those metaphors for life. I could just talk to you about what I know. I'm a simple woman. Everything about me is simple except for these stretch marks. They lead to hell and back. So when you read this, read it with a simple mind. If you are a frat boy Republican like our president, you probably won't get this, because you don't understand why everyone's not getting into a Range Rover and going out to the country club with their friends.

Sociologists say that people like me have disappeared nowadays. That's not entirely true. We're like Bigfoot. We still around, but you have to go find us. Really, we're tucked away. Maybe they're also trying to hide us. But I refuse to go quietly into that great night. I'm going out the same way I came in. My mother was screaming and cussing when I came in, and I'm going to be screaming and cussing when I go out.

Some people say that I should be put on the endangered species list. You let somebody try to put me in the damned zoo! What they try to do with things that are endangered is to try and breed them. But you can't breed me because those days are done.

I just wish more grandmothers would step up. See, grandmas today are twenty-nine years old. If you're twenty-nine, you don't know the things you know at sixty-eight. So they can't be like me. You've got to get older and understand something. People in my generation remember segregation and the civil rights movement. A lot of what I have

learned came the hard way — through chal-
lenges. Nobody has to struggle no more.
Maybe all these better jobs and benefits have
come with a downside.

THE TEN COMMANDMENTS

If any of you, after you finish this book, say,
"I want to become a Madea," I have some
advice for you. Here are the Ten Command-
ments of Being a Madea, according to me.

1. Keep it real. Say what's on your mind
   when you feel like saying it.
2. Life is hard, so laugh, even in the mo-
   ments when people think stuff ain't
   funny. I have sat in funerals and found
   something to laugh about. But you've
   got to be careful when you do that, because you can laugh too hard. There's a
   very simple secret tip on how to handle
   this very sensitive and dangerous situation, which you will learn later if you
   read on.
3. Eat, live, and die. Don't worry about
   dieting. Don't worry about exercising.
   Whatever comes on, let it stay on.
4. Do unto others before they do
   unto you.
5. If they have done it unto you, and you
   haven't done it to them, do it twice.

6. Pick up sticks. Live richly even if you're poor . . . by eating rich food.
7. Whatever you've done in the past is done, and don't be ashamed of it. As long as it didn't involve animals or children, you're all right. You are with the rest of the world.
8. Stand up straight.
9. You will get better with time.
10. This is the final commandment. Live every day like there is a tomorrow to make it up. Live like every day on this earth, you have a tomorrow to apologize.

■ ■ ■ ■

PART TWO
MADEA'S SECRETS OF
ROMANCE

■ ■ ■ ■

The thing that has made me an expert on romance has been dealing with broke-ass men.
If you're broke and you want to impress me,
you have to do some really creative things.
And, believe me, I have seen *everything.*

HOLD THE FRISBEE

Dating, back in the day, used to be romantic and beautiful. You would go out for a walk in the park. There would be doves and swans flying around, little robins and sparrows. You'd just walk hand in hand, talking and whispering and laughing. Ahh, those were the days.

Nowadays, dating is, you get a phone call at two-thirty in the morning. Somebody says, "What you doing?" You say, "Nothing." He says, "I'm on my way." A couple of minutes after he gets there, he says, "Thank you. I enjoyed that." Two weeks after that, he says, "It ain't my baby." And a year after that, he's in jail for child support. That's dating in America. What happened to romance?

I remember when I was younger, I wanted to go out on a date. My momma and daddy didn't let me go out until I was like seventeen or eighteen. They thought it was going to make me be responsible. But instead, all the frustration built up inside me. I went on my first date — I got buck wild.

I went to the prom with this man who lived next door. Brown. We went to school together, too. He was a colorful character — meaning, he wore more colors in one day than you could find at a gay parade. You take the rainbow flag, the Jamaican flag, and the Brazilian flag and roll it all into one — those are the colors he wore every day. You know, I felt sorry for him because nobody else wanted to talk to him. You needed sunglasses to look at him most of the time. He was way too dark to wear all those colors.

As I said, I met him at school. I was a cheerleader. He was on the football team. But my parents only let me go with him because he lived next door and they liked his family. I got drunk and I wish I wouldn't have, because that night changed my life. I got pregnant. The first date! One time! Messed up! Had a daughter!

I had my little girl — I shouldn't say that — she was a big baby named Cora. She's fifty-two now. But back in the day, I couldn't do nothing. I couldn't go out and party. I had to be watching her every day. This is a very sore subject.

That's why I tell the children all the time

who think it's exciting with all these booty calls, slow down, don't be having sex with all these folks. Shut it down. I do this thing called *klink-klink.* It means "lock down." Don't give up nothing. If these young girls knew how the boys were talking about them, they wouldn't go around doing it with everybody.

I tell these children, wait until you get a little older so you can figure out what you really want. Don't be doing it just because somebody else is doing it. They tell you, "You ain't nothing because you're a virgin." Honey, save that virginity — it's worth a hell of a price. Hold on to it as long as you can.

I had this little girl come up to me and say, "Madea, I have sex with a lot of people because it makes me feel loved." I told her, I said, "Baby, having sex with a lot of people don't make you feel loved — it makes you a ho. And I ain't never met a man who said 'I'm looking for a nice ho to settle down with.'" So shut it down.

Now if you're just so hot that you've got to get some, then what the hell is wrong with a condom? I don't understand why these children will walk around in this day and not use something to protect themselves from AIDS and other stuff.

Don't do it, it's the safest thing. And not

just because of AIDS. If you're looking for a good man, he don't want to know that all his friends and everybody in the neighborhood done had a chance. You're like that old mattress that is being thrown out.

Here's how to get a man, a good man: Don't sleep with him. Women think, "Oh, I'm going to put it on him, he's going to love me, I'm going to put it on him." What you don't understand, honey, is that if you're putting it on him, somebody else is going to put it on him and somebody else and somebody else — and, believe it or not, it ain't all that different from you to somebody else. You may think that you're all that special, but the only way you can be special is *to hold out.*

Let me tell you, making love and having sex will get you dinner and a movie. That's all you're going to get out of it. But holding out will get you diamonds and furs and Cadillacs and marriage proposals. A man likes a challenge. If you're throwing it at him, sometimes he don't want to catch it.

I had an old dog, and we would throw the Frisbee at him across the street. He'd run out there and grab it and bring it back. And we'd do that every day. About the fourth or fifth time we'd throw the Frisbee, he'd turn around and look at me and put his head down. You get my drift? Stop throwing your Frisbee! If you want the dog to keep getting the Frisbee, don't throw it too much.

The more you make the man wait, the more special he thinks you are. I remember when I was in school, there was this little girl who slept with the whole football team. I'm sure they sat around the locker room and talked about her like she was a dog. "We had her, you can have her, too." "You want her. Give me two dollars, I'll go get her." She was what they called an expensive ho. Two dollars was high, but she did it. Do you want people talking about you like that? Do you want people talking about you when they see you coming, they say, "Loaded bus — everybody done been on"? Do you want those kinds of titles? They say "ho, ho, ho," and it ain't even Christmas. Are you Santa Claus? Close your legs.

What you want them to be able to say about you is, "Oh, no, man, they ain't nobody getting to that, ain't nobody getting to that." "No, she's something special." That's what you want. Put up the challenge and you can get any man you want. Because any man who's worth his salt wants a challenge.

All these women wondering why they go out on a date and the man ain't calling in three days, he's not calling when he says he's going to call — baby, it's really simple. The man ain't interested. If he wanted you, he'd call you. And all these women sitting saying, "We've been dating all these years, when are you going to marry me?" If you've got a man saying to you, "We're going to get married one day, we're going to get married one day," do you know what he's doing? This may hurt your feelings, but I'm going to be really honest. He's just waiting to see what else is out there, if something better is going to come along. If nothing better comes along in the next few years, you may have a shot at marrying him. That's what he's telling you. Don't put up with that. You are worth more than that, honey.

I believe in *the power.* Let me explain to you what *the power* is. *The power* is the gift that a lot of women don't know they have. See, all women are born with the same special power. When the doctor pulls them out and pats them on their behind and says, "It's a girl," that lets you know you were born with a powerful weapon. Now, you can use your weapon for good or you can use your weapon for bad. But whatever you do, use your weapon, the power of your weapon. Let the force be with you!

Hold the Frisbee.

THE MYSTERY AND THE
WISDOM OF FLIRTING

What I've learned about flirting, you have to be, number one, sexy. Don't try to flirt and you're tow-up. That's crazy as hell.

I don't know why it always is that ugly men always flirt with me. But there's a secret about ugly men, and I'll tell you about that later. If you've got one, hold him close until you read about me talking about them. Don't throw him away just yet. There is some very valuable information coming up that you would pay good money to hear.

Here's how to flirt: Sometimes you've got to go put on your shortest dress and your longest hair. And when you put on your shortest dress, please leave some mystery in it. That's the difference between a miniskirt and a ho-skirt. A ho-skirt shows your Frisbee. A miniskirt shows just enough to cause some mystery. What these young women lack is mystery.

Don't try to compete with these young things — these nineteen- or twenty-year-olds with these low-rise jeans trying to flirt with their men. Because nine times out of ten, if you look anything like me, you're going to look like you just couldn't get your pants up. There will be a sideways smile running up your back. So, please, get out of these lowrider jeans — leave it for the young folk.

You have something over these young women in flirting that they don't have — wisdom. You've got wisdom and class — so use it. A man wants a woman with wisdom who knows how to throw her Frisbee.

See, these teenagers today don't know nothing about mystery and wisdom. You know, you can't walk into a club with a thong on and a string and talk about that you've got mystery. Everybody can look at you and see that you're a ho. Put something on. Cover yourself up. Get some mystery in your flirting. Make it clear when you're flirting with somebody that you're trying to get his attention. Make sure he knows you're in the room but he ain't looking at you for all the wrong reasons. "Oh, look at that — she's special — I've got to meet her." That's what you want him saying. Not "Look at that ho's thong!"

I put a thong on a few months ago trying to be sexy. I've been looking for it but ain't seen it since.

Put on something that smells good — your best perfume, but don't overdo it. Spray it up in the air and walk under it. I can't stand to smell a woman who was on the elevator three days before I got on it. Perfume is supposed to enhance, not cover up or create. It leaves a nice fragrance so we remember your scent. Not "Damned, what the hell was that!"

Flirting for me is in the hips. If you know how to move your hips, from right to left, you will make a man start to wonder, "If she can walk like that, what else can she do like that?" Don't gyrate and jump up and down. And, please, put on some support hose to make sure that everything ain't jiggling all over everyplace. That is so nasty, like you have a waterfall running down your back every time you walk under your clothes. See, I got to the age now that every right and left there's a wiggle that goes all the way down to my calves. But, see, back in the day, when things were tight and right, I could walk into a room and hit bam-bam-bam — everybody would see me. It's all in the way you move. But when you're older, please don't move like that. That bam-bam-bam will cause you to have to have hip-replacement surgery.

Flirting is an attitude. It's a lightness, it's a wonder, it's a mystery. When you flirt, own the room. It ain't a thought. It ain't something you necessarily got to think about how to do it. If you got it, you got it.

How do you let on that you're interested? It depends on where your situation is at that time. If you're trying to get somebody for a night, then you ain't got time for all of the flirting. You just lay it all out on the table where they are and say, Look . . . I'm available. . . . Do you know how to play Frisbee?

But if you're looking for someone who's going to be around longer than that, then you have to play the game. Get a little mystery. Do special things. I like to buy stuff for people. I send them a drink or something. "Hey, see me over here?" You know, get a conversation going. I don't mind spending a little change on something that I want for the long term. For the short term, I ain't spending no money, though.

I'm an aggressive woman. So, if I scare the man off by being aggressive, he sure as hell ain't going to be able to handle me in the bed. Because this Frisbee can go a long, long way. That's okay if the man goes away. Sometimes you got to weed through twenty before you get to the real one who ain't intimidated by an assertive woman who's got *the power.*

THE ART OF THE DANCE

Dancing is an art — you know, especially for black people. We have rhythm. I've seen a lot of people dance over the years. I'm not talking about no waltz or the Lindy Hop. I'm talking about real dancing that comes through us, takes us back to Africa, where you have the stripes across your face . . . your breasts painted and nose pierced.

You know, I used to do this African dance back in the day, me and Josephine Baker. That's right, we were in a play together. She made me mad one night, so I ate all those bananas she used to wear. So she went out there with peels and slipped down. Then my career was over for some reason, because she thought she was the star. I was just the under-under-understudy. That's why she went to Paris. But, anyway, back to dancing.

Dancing is very important. It's important to be able to lose yourself. No matter where you dance, in the church, on the dance floor, wherever it's going on, get out there and lose yourself. And it's a good form of exercise, too. It's enjoying yourself. Most of the time, it's looking like a damned fool. If you really want to laugh, go to a club, sit in the corner, and just watch people dance. And if you really want to bust your gut laughing, watch white people dance to black music. There ain't nothing like watching a whole bunch of white people dancing to Jay-Z.

Dancing is also a form of flirting. So if you don't know how to flirt or what else to do, just ask the man to dance with you. You know, you can tell a lot about people when you're dancing with them. From good dancers you can tell how good they are in the bed. If they've got the right moves in the hips and the ankles, you know you're in for a nice treat. But if they're gyrating like they're having a seizure and they can't catch the rhythm of the beat, you know they won't be able to catch the rhythm of the stroke. That's somebody you don't want to necessarily dance with . . . or play Frisbee.

UGLY SEXOCOLOGY

I told you I was going to give you some valuable information about ugly people. Well, now that we're talking about flirting and dancing, let's continue in that same realm, because ugly people fit right in. You'll be sitting in a club and the ugliest person in there will be sending you drinks and talking to you. I used to ignore these people. I used to give them a hard time. I wouldn't give them the time of day until one night when I was really, really lonely. The club was closing up, and there were only a few people left. And one of them was this ugly man who was buying me drinks all night. So, I say, what the hell. I was in a bad situation. I just broke up with my man. You know, after enough Hennessey, Bernie Mac will start looking like Denzel Washington.

Anyway, I got to talking to him. He wasn't too bad — we held a pretty decent conversation. You know, we got to know each other well and went out a few more times. But I would never go nowhere with him in public because, child, the man was ugly. I ain't wanted nobody saying, "She's desperate as hell if she's with that ugly man."

But what I found out about people who are ugly, here it is. This is the secret. Get ready. Grab a pen and get your phone book and mark an asterisk by all the ugly people in the book. Here's what you need to know. They know that if they get one shot at having you, they've got to put it on you in every way that they can. So they have to know what they're doing — they have to have a million years of practice. They have to get their degree in ugly sexocology. If they get you in bed, they know that they have to *wear you out.*

I have learned to appreciate and thank God for ugly men. They will have you speaking another language. They are incredible. If you don't believe me, find the ugliest one that you can. Write me and let me know if I was right. Child, pretty soon I didn't care that he was ugly. I wanted to go everywhere with him. His name was Dr. Feel-good. So, the next time you run into somebody who's ugly, give him a break! They might break you!

It's like that old calypso song, "If you want to be happy the rest of your life, make an ugly woman your wife." The same goes for your husband. "If loving you is wrong, then I don't want to be right." If loving your ugly self is wrong, then I don't want to be right in the sight of nobody because you know what you're doing!

You may be attached to someone who's pretty, who looks beautiful, but what I've found out is that it's only going to last for as long as that feeling lasts. Lust don't last. Lust don't take you past two weeks . . . unless he's ugly. And pretty people usually don't have to do nothing. They're the kind of folk that just like to lay there. That ain't me. Get yourself a dirty-fingernail, back-scrubbing mechanic that looks like King Kong, and I promise you, you will be happy.

So the next time you see somebody walking down the street with an ugly man, especially if it's a girlfriend of yours, give her a high five. "Go ahead, baby, I'm trying to find me one, too!"

■ ■ ■ ■

PART THREE
MADEA ON LOVE AND
MARRIAGE

(OFTEN TWO COMPLETELY
SEPARATE TOPICS)

■ ■ ■ ■

The reason I want to talk about marriage and love is that so many people want a financier instead of a fiancé.

THE SECRET FOR A GOOD RELATIONSHIP

I don't think it is a secret. It's just plain and simple *communication.* You have to be able to talk. Communication is very important, not only in a marriage and relationships. In anything you're going through, you've got to be able to communicate. On the scale of one to ten, communication is about an eleven and a half.

Here's another thing I've learned: If you want to marry somebody and have a good relationship, the minute it starts to get good is when you stop waiting for people to do what you want them to do. You don't think alike. You're on two different levels, two different playing fields. You have to *tell* them what you want them to do most of the time. Nine times out of ten, they'll get it right. But don't be hurt when somebody doesn't do what you would have done. You can't never expect people to do what you would do.

The next thing on the list is *keep your eyes open.* A lot of folks don't want to pay attention to the signs. When you see a stop sign, if you don't stop, you will run through it, get a ticket, probably have an accident, and kill somebody. Pay attention to the signs. When you see a sign that something is wrong, you need to address it. If you feel like the man or woman is cheating, somewhere inside is nagging you — that is a sign. And if you think it, they're probably doing it. So you have to pay attention. Don't be a fool. Don't sit there and sleep when you feel something is going on. Don't ignore it. Speak on it. You ask questions. I know you're thinking: He's going think I'm nagging, he's going think I'm pestering him. I don't give a damn if he thinks you're nagging him or pestering or whatever. If you feel it, ask. It's the only way you're going to feel better. Ask the questions.

If that's your marriage . . . that's your husband who you are trying to keep — excuse me, men, but I'm talking to women right now. If that's your husband, and you're trying to keep him, you need to not be afraid to ask the questions. The thing that pisses me off is that you've done spent all that time training the man on how to be a good man for you, had him all of these years, almost like training a puppy. Now that you have a full-grown dog — you taught him how to catch the Frisbee — here comes some little pussycat trying to take him from you. That makes me want to fight. That makes me want to go and beat the hell out of them if I catch them.

But if you're watching and paying attention, I'm not saying the man ain't going to cheat, but please don't make it easy for him. Pay attention to that little voice inside.

I can't understand these folks sit around and say they ain't never seen it coming. "I didn't know it was coming . . . we've been married twenty years . . . and he just up and walked out." To hell with that! There were signs all along if you opened the door a little bit. You just refused to pay attention to him because you're living in your own world.

I'm an old-school fool. That means I go through wallets, check cell phone records, bank statements, time cards, pay stubs. I make sure that my man is where he says he's going to be. I even make sure his paycheck goes to me, and he ain't bringing it to some little hussy. If he gets mad, then that's his problem. You ain't being nosy, you're just doing what the Bible says. Watch so you don't have to fight, and keep praying.

He's going to think you're nagging, but you sit there and keep asking questions. Pay attention to your intuition. Hold on for a second. Put a pin in this. I'm going to come back and talk about this. Intuition deserves a whole chapter by itself.

Until Death Did We Part

I love marriage. I believe in the sanctity of marriage. I believe in keeping a marriage going up until the point that it gets on your damned nerves. Then shut it down. I don't understand all these people trying to stay together for life. You know, if you're staying together for life and it's working, you love that person and you're best friends, that's great. But if you're with somebody who's crazy as hell so you can stay together for life, that's stupid as hell.

Back in my day, that's what you did. I was married eight times, and I stayed with every one of my husbands for life, for *their* lives. You see, they all died of mysterious causes after some terrible arguments. I am often asked with all the husbands I've had who the real love of my life was. They often guess that it was the one with the shiny teeth. But I think because the way I was raised I never could really have love for one man. I always loved something about each one. When that thing wore out, like teeth or pretty hair or good skin, it was time for a change. I could

58

never find one that had everything. That's why after they worked on my nerves, they disappeared!

You see, the only thing all my husbands had in common was that they had the opportunity to eat my famous sweet potato pie. It always works. After they eat it, three days later, you won't hear a word or a peep.

I can only assume that there will be many people after reading this who will want to get a copy of my recipe for sweet potato pie. It is a secret recipe. And the good news is that I will never ever be sent to jail, because no coroner in the world will ever figure out what's in this pie. The great thing about my sweet potato pie is that it works for me. Now you have to figure out what's going to work for you in your sweet potato pie. In other words, I'm not giving you the recipe. I refuse to, on the grounds that it may incriminate me. I'm pleading the Fifth Dimension and Marilyn McCoo.

Maybe in the future, I'll come out with a cookbook, and I might change my mind and put in the recipe for sweet potato pie. However, it will have to be encrypted and encoded. You would have to read in between the lines.

Again, if you don't understand something I'm saying here and you're not black, you will have to ask somebody who is. If you happen to be a black person reading this and you don't get it, oh, well, you've spent too much time away from your culture. Come home — we miss you.

Marriage is a wonderful thing when it's working. But you've got to make sure you're getting married for the right reasons. When you're young, you get married for silly reasons. I remember one time I got married because the man had pretty teeth. You know, back in my day, you didn't see too many men with pretty teeth. They had gold or two or three of them missing. You didn't know whether to smile at them or kick a field goal. So this one with the pretty teeth, we got into an argument one night and he lost all them teeth, and I didn't want him no more.

The next husband I had was for another stupid reason. . . . Well . . . you know . . . it's hard to talk about him. He had a good job. He had benefits. I'll marry a man with benefits in a minute. That means you can go to a doctor, you ain't got to go to the county hospital — you can go to a nice hospital. You can get your teeth done, all your health stuff done. You even have access to what they call four hundred and one Ks. So I married him because I wasn't feeling too well and I needed to have some feminine stuff done. So

I stayed with him for as long as I needed to get everything done. When I got well enough to walk on the sidewalk, I kicked him to the curb.

Here's another stupid reason to get married: you want a wedding! Do you know that there are people who are in love with the idea of having a wedding? Some of these young girls have already bought the dress, picked out the ring, the bridesmaids, and everything — and they don't even have the man yet. All they want is the wedding. What they need to do in those kinds of situations is have a party, hell!

You talking about a wedding, you better make sure you're planning it for the rest of your life, because some of these fools are crazy. But if you find the right one and you all match tit for tat and you can be around that person twenty-four hours a day, seven days a week, and they don't get on your nerves — then you're ready for marriage. But you're going to need to be around them for more than a year. You need to see people in all kinds of seasons to make sure that the seasons that they walk in agree with your seasons. Ain't nothing like seeing one person in summer and the other in winter and they're trying to get along.

Another reason not to get married right

away: I don't believe in love at first sight . . .
I believe in *lust* at first sight. So what you
need to do is give yourself time. I have a
ninety-day rule. If you're still in love and enjoying being with the person in ninety days,
then you need to date six more months. Give
the person at least a year before you make
the decision — and not a year of you all living in separate cities, but looking at each
other every day.

CHEATING ON YOUR SPOUSE

After you've done all of this, you've got your
man, you figured out it's going to work,
everything's wonderful and great, then you
need some tips on how to keep your marriage spicy. The best way to keep your marriage spicy is to cheat! I'm just kidding!
Don't go out there running around saying
that Madea's saying to cheat. No, here's
what you do: Cheat with your husband or
your wife. If you're wondering how do you
cheat with your spouse — a wig, a pair of
high heels, and a street corner can sure make
a difference in your relationship. I'm telling
you, when you're doing something that you
ain't got no business doing, something that's
taboo, it can make it feel like it's better than
it really is.

Here is how I kept one of my marriages

spicy. My husband and I used to play this game called Pimps Up, Ho's Down, where I was the ho and he was the pimp. We meet out on the corner . . . I'd have my ho clothes on — we almost got arrested one time. He'd come in his old Cadillac and pick me up. I wouldn't get in the car for less than thirty dollars. Even if it's your husband, don't get into the car for less than thirty dollars. You don't want to be a cheap ho. So he'd pay the money, and we'd go to a motel and have a good time. We did that for about six months.

You've got to be careful when you give a man a fantasy, because sometimes they'll take it too damned far. After about six months, I was tired of it, and he was getting a little rough — he was taking that pimp thing a little too far. I mean, I was making some money, but not enough to put up with all that. So we had to stop playing that game.

Then we started playing another game where he would pick me up in the supermarket. I'd go in to get the groceries, and he'd come up to me and start talking to me and say, "What's your name?" He'd be following me around and everybody in the supermarket would be looking at us. Then I'd go up to the checkout counter and he'd say, "Can I get your phone number? I want to take you home." I'd give him my phone number, and the lady who was ringing me up would look at me like I was crazy. You won't believe this. One time I had some freak ask if she could come, too!

MARRYING SOMEONE LIKE YOUR PARENTS

Marriage is a wonderful thing unless you marry someone like your parents. Now, if you were lucky and had a good father or a good mother, then it's okay to marry someone like your parents. But if your parents were crazy as hell, please don't marry them. Nine times out of ten, you do.

Most of the time when a woman is looking at a man, she's looking through the eyes of what her father was. Her father is like a glass lens between her and the man she's looking at — whoever the father was and how he behaved, that's how she's going to judge the man she's interested in. You've got to be really careful with that.

My daddy was nice after he got hit in the head with the log, but in his younger days he was a man who liked to fight and argue. So, initially, when I went out looking for men, that's what I was attracted to. If a man wasn't fighting and arguing, then he wasn't no man. When I ran up on a good, kind, nice one, I didn't know how to treat him because I was looking at him through the glass that was my father. But I've got some advice. Instead, try really hard to take your father out of the equation and look at that person for who he is, what he came through and look at his family situation.

What I also found out is that when you marry someone, you didn't know that you don't marry just that person. No, you marry the whole family and the family history. Now, me, for instance, I almost married a nice man named Willie Humphrey. Back then, I didn't even know too much about my own family because my father had a bunch of children outside of the house — and it turned out Willie Humphrey was my brother! They told us we were in the South, so it was okay. But I didn't feel it would be right. I didn't want to be raising my nephew as my child.

So when you're about to marry somebody, learn his whole family history. Just don't talk to the person about who he is. Talk to the momma and the daddy and the sisters and the brothers and the uncles and the next-door neighbors. You need to be an FBI agent before you marry that person. You want dental records and tests for all kinds of stuff like schizophrenia, venereal diseases, heart disease, and diabetes. You want to know every bit of information you can. Credit reports.

Find out what his score is. All of that matters! Talk to the employees who he works with. As a matter of fact, go back and talk to the kindergarten teacher and ask how was his first day at school. Did he cry or did he stand there and be a man? All of that information is important when you're thinking about marrying somebody — especially if that person is like your parents!

You know, it comes down to a point where you need to stop looking at your spouse or boyfriend to be your parent and to validate you and give you everything your parents didn't. You got to go get that stuff for yourself. You got to wake up every day and say, "I'm good enough, I deserve to be happy, I deserve to have all this good stuff coming my way." You can't depend on that to come from nobody else.

I tell people, don't go out there trying to get no relationship when you ain't ready. Hell, sit back and work on yourself. How are you going to offer something to somebody else if you ain't been to visit *you* yet?

TRUST YOUR INTUITION

Before you can even read this section, there are some questions you need to ask yourself:

Am I a paranoid person? If the answer is yes, please go to the next section.

Am I a person that's just crazy? If so, next section.

If you said yes to either of these questions, your intuition is off base. You're not going to be able to enjoy this. As a matter of fact, you don't even understand what the hell I just said.

If you are chemically imbalanced or you got any drug inducement or you are close to a certain few days of the month, please, don't necessarily trust your judgment or intuition. Or if you're pregnant, everything is going to make you cry and make you sensitive. Intuition is really out of balance when you're around these areas of your life.

So I would like to talk to the normal, regular people. Now, you got to be honest with yourself if you're going to do this test. If you're a normal, regular person who wakes up happy every day — you ain't got to take no pills to get up or take no pills to go to bed. If you feel something telling you, kicking you, "hmm, hmm, something ain't right," then listen up! You're the person I'm talking to. You're the person who's sensitive to your intuition, and I can teach you to be even more sensitive. I can train you to really pay attention.

Still yourself. Get the kids out of the house, let the man go to work, and get into a silent place. You could even be cleaning up and still just be quiet and listen. Turn off everything in the house. No distractions. Some people are afraid of silence because of the things they might hear. If you turn everything off, including that chatter in your brain, your intuition will start to talk to you. Especially if you're cleaning the house and going through your man's pockets! It will really show you something.

For example, he says he's going to work, and something's saying, "No, no, that ain't right." I tell you, if that happens, you have to be on it. Nine times out of ten, that little thing that tells you that something's going on is telling you right.

If that alarm is going off in me, I get a little tingle. It starts not in my body, but in my purse. I can look inside my bag at my pistol, and it seems to have a slight vibration. And I say, "Hmmm! Something is going on somewhere!" But normal people usually get a little tingle in their body that something is upset in them — it ain't a physical sickness but it's something that just gnaws you and says, "Something's not right." Any fool can see when something don't make sense. If you pay attention to it, that little thing will keep you out of trouble, out of accidents, out of marriage trouble, out of your kid's trouble. It will tell you everything that's going on. But you've got to pay attention to it.

If your man is telling you nothing's going on and he's getting all upset and starts screaming and fussing, then you know you've hit a nerve. That means something is going on! "Why are you always questioning me? Why you asking me this? You don't trust me?" The answer to all of these questions should be "hell no" if you're paying attention to your intuition. If it was not true, he'd just let it pass. He would say, "Hey, baby, that ain't it," and just move on. He wouldn't be screaming and fussing and yelling for days.

Watch out, too, for what men do. I call it *turning it around.* You catch him at something, and he starts acting like it's you. If you've got the kind of man who's jealous — everywhere you go, he wants to know, somebody smiles at you and he gets mad. I hate to be the one to tell this to you. The only reason he's doing it is that he's got a few women on the side. He doesn't want you to do what he's doing. And he certainly does not want you to run into him nowhere with any of his women.

Even if you're walking down the street and somebody asks you for directions, or you're walking to your car late at night on a dark street, and your intuition says, "Hurry up, speed up, get into the car, shut this door, run this light," pay attention to all of that stuff, because it's telling you that for a reason.

If you ask a question and your intuition says, "No, that ain't the right answer," your intuition should say to you, "Ask another question." If that ain't the right answer either, keep asking questions until your intuition tells you, "He has just told you the truth."

You've always got to listen between the words. If somebody says one thing to you and you listen between what they're saying, you usually can get the answer. The great thing about liars is that if they tell you a lie, they keep telling lies to cover the last thing they said. So if you keep asking questions, you're going to get a whole lot of lies. Then you wait a week and go back and ask the same questions (after you write up all the answers to those other lies). If they don't match, then you've caught them in the lie. Your intuition was right. There are all kinds of tests for intuition.

I don't care if somebody gets mad because I'm asking so many questions. Get mad, you can get the hell out of my house if I can't ask you no questions about where you're going and where you've been. (This is again only for normal people. If you're crazy, please don't do this.) Ask the questions until you feel good about the answers. It's just like those game shows where the buzzer goes *ammpppp!* You'll see a big red X in front of you when you get the wrong answer. From now on, every time you ask a question of somebody and you want to know the answer — and they give you the wrong answer — you're going to see this big old red X in your mind. Keep asking questions until Vanna turns you a letter!

SECRET TIPS FOR ENDING A RELATIONSHIP

There ain't no secret tips for ending a relationship. The best way to do it is to be direct. Please don't have nobody hanging on, wondering what's going on and why you ain't calling. If you don't want to be bothered, tell them, "Hell, I don't want to be bothered." Unless that person is like Ike Turner!

There are people you have to be really careful with on how you let them down. Because if a man is doing something wrong to you over and over and over again, please don't just all at once get mad. That's not the way to do it. If he's doing something wrong, question it, get it right every time he does it, so that it won't be that he does all of this big stuff — then one day he does a little thing — and you been holding all of this stuff inside — you get mad as hell and blow up. And he's wondering, what the hell did he do because you didn't tell him all along.

Sometimes, when you're training a puppy, you have to put his nose into what he did for him to understand not to do it again. You get my drift? Some men are like puppies. Put his nose in what he did so he knows not to do it again. If he keeps doing it, then you might need to get a cat.

So, if you do as I say, you won't explode, and he'll understand when you put him out the door.

I've got the best motto for dealing with relationships. Let a man make a million mistakes because they ain't perfect. Just don't let them make the same mistake over and over and over again. Before you end the relationship, let people be human. Let the man make the mistake. Don't ask for anybody to be perfect because you ain't perfect, either. Try everything you can to make it work, especially if you've got a good one.

This is the tip for getting rid of a crazy man. Here's what you do. Be extremely careful. The first thing you need to do is move. Find a new job. Transfer to a new city. It might be just what you need. Dye your hair.

Change your name. Get into a witness-protection program. Go start a new life because if you've got a crazy man it's hard as hell to get rid of him. But some of this is your fault. You knew he was crazy the first day that you met him and gave him your phone number. You know how you knew? I'll tell you. If you gave him your number at three o'clock and by four o'clock he filled up your voice mail, you should have known then not to call him anymore.

If all else fails, there is one very drastic method that should only be used when there are no other options. It should have a little warning label attached to it, but here goes: If the man is nuts and he's stalking you and doing all sorts of crazy things, *the best thing to do is get crazier than him.* I leave the rest to your imagination. That way I take no responsibility for your funeral.

REGRETS?

Regrets in my life? I regret Brown, that was Cora's daddy. I felt like I was wrestling with a polar bear that night. I thought I was grown. I've never in my life understood what happened that night, but it was only one night — I didn't like him then, and I don't like him now. I always told Cora that her daddy went off to war and he was over in

World War II and he died. But I finally had to come clean and tell her, because she knew Brown, had known him all her life, used to laugh at him and talk about him like a dog. So I finally had to tell her that Brown was her dad. If I have any regrets, it's him being her daddy. I wouldn't give her back to where she came from because it sure would hurt like hell. But I sure in hell would take back that night.

I believe that everything that happens to you can work together for your good because I believe everything you deal with in this life is all for a reason and is supposed to make you a better person. If you're sitting in a chair and you get uncomfortable, you're going to move somewhere else. That's how life is. You get to a place where you're comfortable — and suddenly all these things start happening to make you feel uncomfortable. I'm not talking about things to make you depressed or tear you down — that's where most folk get messed up — they get depressed, suicidal, strung out on drugs.

What this discomfort is really designed to do is get you to move into a better place — your destiny, the next place you're supposed to be. So if all hell breaks loose, I have to look at me and figure out, okay, what I am supposed to be doing? Looks like I'm supposed to be moving to another place. So I'll get up and make that move, and then it will get a little easier and more comfortable.

TELLING A FRIEND THEY'RE IN LOVE WITH A BIG MISTAKE

I tell parents who ask, "Madea, what should I do about this? . . . What should I do about that?" I tell them all the time, if your child's out there doing something crazy, there ain't too much you can do. What you got to do is take care of you. Once you've raised that child or given them the best advice you can, that's all you can do. This is what I tell parents.

If you see your child with someone who's terrible and you're jumping up and down acting the fool — "I don't want you to see this person" — you're going make that child want that person more, because you're making it more dangerous than it is. What you got to do is stop doing that and sit back and say, "If that's who you want, bring him over for dinner. Let's all go out. Let's sit down and talk."

Even though you can't stand him, sit there and play the game with him. What that's going to do is give you a lot of different options and ideas. You get a chance to really see what's going on. That way, you're letting your child know that it's okay. See, that child won't have no pressure from you. That child can make up his or her own mind. But if you say "no, no, no," they'll stay with that person just to defy you. Trust me!

So nine times out of ten, you try to get involved in it. Don't push it away. Get involved in it, no matter how bad you think it is, so you can be there when the child needs you, number one.

WHEN THINGS GO BEYOND DENIAL

There was this lady in Detroit who just got killed by this man who killed her and her three daughters. She was crying out for help. She wrote this poem, "Why Do You Love Me?" And all the people in the neighborhood knew that this man was beating this woman, and nobody offered any help to her. If you see it, at least offer to help. Don't sit there and say, "Well, I ain't going to say something because she might get mad." To hell with them getting mad — they'll thank you later.

Your friend's coming to work with black eyes and she's late — you know what's going on. Her arm's broken the next week. Pull her to the side and say, "Look, I can help you get some help. Here's my phone number. You call me if you need some help." If they get mad at you, you've done your part. If something happens, you don't want that on your conscience — "I should have said something."

If you're lying in your house and you hear your neighbors fussing and screaming and arguing — you're going to lie there and turn over and go to sleep or turn the TV up? No! Call the police. I don't care if they get mad. They shouldn't be over there doing it. Next time, they'll think before they do it. Get involved. People don't get involved no more. Back in the day, that's how we raised our children and kept our neighborhood right. That's how we kept the drug dealers out. We all stuck together. We got involved. They call it "nosy" now. You know, they got people living in subdivisions on the same block for years that don't even know each other.

One time, somebody came up to me to tell me something about a man I was messing around with. And you know what? I got mad. "Don't be telling me nothing about my man! I don't want you telling me nothing." I went off. And that's what's going to happen. Just get ready for it. As soon as you tell people their man or woman is doing something, they're going to kick you to the curb. But they're going to come back as soon as they see it. You see, when they told me, the first thing that happened was, my antennas went up. I started watching, and I started seeing things on my own. So I was glad they said something to me in the long run, but I wasn't glad right then. We made up a little while later.

Everybody's got denial going on. Nobody wants to hear the truth, especially when you're in your own world. Now, be prepared. Sometimes when you tell somebody something, they will go back and tell the man or woman what you said. Then they call you up, cussing you out. See, I like drama. Let them come with some foolishness. I'll be ready to tear the place up.

■ ■ ■ ■

PART FOUR
KIDS!

(ENOUGH SAID)

■ ■ ■ ■

The reason I want to write about kids is this:
If you don't have these tidbits of information, they will kill you. So this chapter is to
help you kill them first.

THE BEAUTY OF CHILDBIRTH

Childbirth — I've heard it called a beautiful, wonderful, extraordinary thing. I know women who have said they didn't want any drugs — natural childbirth. I don't know what the hell they were talking about or what kind of baby they had. Maybe their baby was two pounds.

My baby, Cora, was a big baby. I think she was about 98 pounds when she was born. I was about 380 myself. And you know, I ain't been able to take the weight off ever since the day she came, but that's just fifty-two years now. Every time I look in the mirror, I say, "Damn, when did that happen?" You ever just look at yourself and you got so much weight, you don't know where it came from? When did it sneak up on you? I walked past the mirror the other day and almost scared myself to death — I was getting ready to go into the shower. I said, "Who in the hell is that looking back at me?" You know, I stepped on my nipple — I thought somebody had pinched me. Well, that's all from childbirth. I'm glad she's here, but I regret it every day.

She's still big, my Cora. I look at her and say, "Look at my little fat baby." She was so lumpy. But pretty as she could be, just a little butterball. I used to just roll her down . . . I didn't buy a stroller. I would just roll her down the street like a ball.

They didn't have epidurals back when I had Cora. I wish they did. I just lay there and screamed, "Leave it in, hell, because it's hurting too much to come out. Just leave it in there." She would have taken her SAT from the womb.

People want to know what was childbirth like? Well, here's one easy way to describe it: I have a pair of pliers and I go down your throat and pull out your intestines, little bit by little bit, while telling you to push at the same time. That's what it feels like.

Postpartum depression — yes, I've had it for fifty-two years. That's why I only had one because I've been depressed ever since then. Depression is a pretty common and serious problem, so I'll go into a little more detail about it later on.

If there was another way for me to have a

baby — I like this surrogate mother thing, where you pay some other woman to go through all that hell. I know that some people really don't have a choice. But if I had a choice, that's what I would do. I would give her my baby to carry so I could have kept my body intact. I was real sexy back then. I ain't been able to get that sexy again.

THE SINGLE MOTHERS' CLUB

This is very useful information that I hope will make you enjoy your life more and be a happier parent. If you're a single mother, you should give this very serious thought. It was out of necessity, so I wouldn't go crazy that I got together with the other single women in the neighborhood. I was sitting around one night when Cora was little and thinking how badly I wanted to go out. I called a girlfriend who said, "I want to go out, too, but I got kids." I called another who said the same thing. All of us wanted to go out. What came out of it was that we formed our single mothers' club.

It's really not rocket science. Hell, cave women must have thought up the same thing. This club just meant that on certain nights somebody would have to stay with the kids. Whoever watched the kids the last time, we would pay for everything for them when we went out. But of course, we had a two-drink minimum because I wasn't going to be spending all my hard-earned stripping and insurance money from killing husbands to buy drinks for some broad.

It was a lot of fun. The more women joined, the more fun it became — except of course when there was somebody in there who wasn't supposed to be there, and they'd start a whole bunch of mess and we'd kick them out and their child. You got to be careful to just get good people in there who want to have a good time.

Being able to go out for a night and let your hair down for a night was just what the doctor ordered. Back in the day, we had slow music. At the end of an evening, you could slow dance with a guy. I call that a "test-drive" to see how well they move. These children don't test-drive no more (that's why they have so many kids). After you've done the test-drive, you decide you want to bring him home overnight.

So if you want to form a local chapter of Madea's Single Mothers' Club, here's what you do: You get ten women together in your neighborhood — ten women with some sense. Make sure they ain't got no crazy-ass man. They're single by themselves with one child each or two children — if they've got

five or six, then they can't be in the club —
they need to learn to keep their legs closed.
You all take turns sharing the children with
each other while you go out, so you can all
enjoy your life.

You see, before I got smart and formed this
club, I didn't have a life. Every time I wanted
to go out, my momma would meet me at the
door with the baby and say, "Wherever
you're going, you're going to have to
take her."

I couldn't say, "Momma, keep the baby,
I'm going —" I couldn't even finish the sen-
tence before she'd say, "You're grown up
enough to lay there and have her, you're
grown up enough to take care of her." So
everywhere I went, here come Cora . . . big
old Cora, right there on my hip. She was a
big baby. I had to take the child to work. I
took the child to my graduation on my hip.

So form this club and have everybody take
responsibility for each other. While four girl-
friends will go out one night, one girlfriend
will be home watching the children. Rotate it
every week. It will be a great way for you all
to form a support group for the children, for
the single mothers, and to go out and have a
good time every once in a while.

Again, the voice of experience wants to tell
you loud and clear: When you form your

club, make sure that one of you ain't a crazy woman. When you form your circle, close it. Make sure that everyone has a psychological evaluation. You don't need to go to a doctor. Just notice if the children are crazy as hell, dirty, and cussing at the mouth, then you know you don't want that mother watching your children. Their children have to be able to respect them, so they can be a member of the club. Take a vote on who you want to allow into the club. I think it's a good idea. You should try it. It might work. If it don't — oh, well, this is for entertainment purposes only.

THE BAG OF BELTS

My tip for raising your beautiful bundle of joy, making them a successful product into society, a wonderful citizen, is a little three-word tip that my parents passed on to me and I'd like to pass on to you: *Whup that ass.*

I look at some of these children that don't got no discipline and no home training because their parents are sitting around trying to be the child's friend. To hell with being your child's friend! Even if you're all close in age, you still got to be the parent. These days, children need guidance. Somebody has to stand up and say, "What in the hell are you doing?" Somebody's got to be the fear factor for them.

My first whupping from my momma? I think I was eight days old. I was crying about something. She popped the hell out of me, and I've never cried since. I think I was hungry and wanted milk, and she didn't feel like it at the time. My mother was a multitask kind of woman when I was growing up. She could throw one breast over her shoulder and feed one child and have the other breast in another room feeding another child. At the same time she could be sewing and washing, playing cards, and having one of my Uncle Johnsons come by, too.

I have a bag of belts that was passed down to me from my momma and my momma's momma. That bag of belts you respected! You could walk in the house and know that you did something wrong if the bag wasn't where it was supposed to be. You knew how bad it was what you did by the selection of the belt for your whupping. So if you was really, really bad and did something really crazy, you got the thick belt with the rhinestones in it.

My worst whupping? Okay, this is what happened. There were two pieces of pie in the kitchen. One was for me, and one was for her. I ate mine and was still hungry. You know, we didn't have pie or sugar that often.

So when she came out of the room with my uncle and didn't see the pie, she went crazy and got the big belt.

What that whupping taught me I put to good use whenever the situation called for it. If you're a parent, tear out these pages to make sure your child doesn't read this. Here's what I learned: If I screamed loud, that meant that I was in a whole lot of pain, and the beatings would last a shorter period of time. But you had to pace yourself when you got these kind of whuppings, because if you screamed too soon, it would make her know you're lying. You had to wait until at least hit number three to start screaming. Hit number four, you start crying. But if she was real mad, it didn't matter. By the time she got to hit number 288, she would be tired. Wait it out.

I don't believe in child abuse. Let me make that perfectly clear. But I do believe in the child getting an ass whupping if something ain't right. Sometime punishment ain't enough. The thing about kids these days is that they're a lot smarter than children were when we were growing up. There are some children you can say, "Go to your room and don't come out till I say so," and that will be enough to straighten them out. The next day they do the right thing. Then there are others that you can put them in the room, lock them up, throw away the key, they'll do the same thing. Those are the kind of kids that need the "whup that ass" adjustment.

You got to adjust your temperature for every child. Each child has to be treated individually. One child might get jealous of the other because you don't whup them. Well, that child doesn't need the spanking and discipline of the other child. It's strange how all these kids can be raised in the same house and each one of them turn out differently.

When you begin to whup that ass, they will begin to act like they got some sense. I believe in that. Now, there's a fine line between whupping that ass and child abuse. The belt is whupping. The buckle is abuse. If you use the buckle, nowadays, children will call 911 on you. So be careful.

Too many people want to be friends with their children. When your child starts paying the bills or brings any money in the house, and starts telling you that you can retire and relax, then you all can sit there and be a friend.

I think it was Dr. Phil who said, "Negotiate with your children." Now, as I understand it, to have a successful negotiation, two parties have to have something the other party wants to have. Am I right? So let me evaluate this.

If I'm negotiating with my child, what the hell do they have to negotiate with? I'm paying all the bills, making all the money, buying the food, putting clothes on them. What does the child have as a bargaining chip, just to behave right? Hell no, you're going to do it right anyway! You're going to do what I say. When you turn eighteen and go out on your own, you can do what the hell you want.

Some people tell me they don't want their child to be afraid of them. I don't understand that. People say, "Calm down and count to ten." No, I'm not counting to ten. I'm going to count to 9-1-1 to call an ambulance, because one of us is getting ready to go to the hospital.

You see, things went well for me, because my child was afraid of me. That's what's wrong with these children today. They have no fear of their parents. When children are afraid, they have some sort of reverence. So when you walk in the room, they're going to stop what they're doing and behave themselves no matter what they were doing. That's respect. That don't come from just being your child's friend or just being somebody who they admire. That comes from knowing that if they go too far, you got all the power and all the tools to bring them back in line.

It's like laws in America. If you break the law, you pay the consequences — the more severe the law, the more severe the consequences. Hell, this country will put you to death for doing something real, real wrong. So when you're raising kids, remember — *you are the law!* Lay the law down and they will respect you.

There are two kinds of children. Some children will do the right thing because they fear their parents, they fear God, and they're just good kids. Then there are the other kids that you need to put the fear of God in. I've learned how to do that through intimidation. Yes, I intimidated my child. I would stand up real close to her. She wouldn't know what I was going to do from day to day. She didn't know what I was going to be mad at, so she was always on her best behavior around me. She thought I was psycho, and some days I thought so, too. But the best part about it, it made her behave.

The great thing about it is that even today — Cora is fifty-two — I could be across the room and just take a look at her — and she'd be doing something wrong — she'd straighten up. She could feel that kind of in- timidation and power. She could be turned totally away from me and would feel the wrath of my eyes on her. The hairs on the back of her neck would stand up. Then she'd get some sense.

Cora ain't get away with nothing. Cora used to go to church every Sunday, and I didn't even go to church. I was wondering why she was going to church all the time. When she got older, she told me. It was because Cora was praying every day that she would be all right growing up in my house. Everything she did, I was on her. You've got to outsmart these kids before they outsmart you.

Here's one other piece of helpful information. Nine times out of ten, they're doing something you've already tried. So how are you going to let them run a game on you when you know what they're doing? There were times I would sit back and know exactly what she was up to and I'd just let her go on and do it. You can't protect your children from everything. Sometimes they need to bump their heads and realize the horror in it themselves. Just don't stand by and let them do things that will destroy their lives forever.

I used to worry about Cora hanging with the wrong people, but I stopped doing it. What I learned early on is that I put so much fear and so much good stuff in my child. When she got old enough to start making her own decisions about who she wanted to be around, all I knew was that I had done all I could and those were choices she was going to have to make. There were a couple of folks that I didn't want her around. Refer back to the first part of the chapter on "telling someone they're in love with a big mistake" for the secret on how to handle this.

My last tip on child raising is this: It's been said by psychologists (not that I know any), they say that from zero to three are the impressionable years of a child — and zero to five is when they form all their personality traits. So that is the time when you have to break that will. Break brute force into submission, get that personality straight during that time. Don't let them get away with nothing at that time. When they have a temper tantrum, you straighten them out. So when they get a little older, they will remember those early years consciously somewhere to keep them straight. I know you're saying, "Who wants to be on a child every day?" After you do that the first years, I promise you, it gets easier because of the groundwork you did early on. Then, all you have to do is what I call "whup that ass" maintenance. Every month or so, just give them a whupping to keep them within the guidelines you have set.

So please take my advice. If you ain't set the rules in place by zero to five, you got hell to pay come sixteen, seventeen, eighteen years old. If you've already messed up, then pass this chapter on to somebody with young kids, so they won't make the same mistakes you did!

MAIDS IN THE HOUSE

When you have children, you have to have rules in the house. Rule number one: If I make a mess, you clean it up. If they break the rules, they have to go through the consequences. If you don't clean up, you don't live here. If you don't wash the dishes, you don't eat. I mean that from the bottom of my heart. I don't have problems getting children to clean up after themselves. If you want to stay here, it's just that simple.

I can't stand to walk into someone's house and their child's room is nasty as hell and the rest of the house is spotless. No, you going to clean up from top to bottom, and I'm going to use you as a mop and a vacuum cleaner if you don't get up there and get it yourself. See, that's what I've learned. There are consequences. For every action, there's a reaction. And what people need to understand about that is that you tell a child to do something, they need to do it.

You have to start early. You can't start telling them at twenty. They have to start at eight days old. As soon as they come home from the hospital, you have to start playing monotone-sounding tapes for them. "You will clean. You will clean. You will clean. You will cook. You will cook." You brainwash them. That's right. That's your child to do whatever you want with. So brainwash them. My Cora was cleaning up so much one time. Everything was almost too spotless. Hell, I thought I must have played that tape too much. And then I thought, Almost too spotless? What the hell am I thinking about?

SIXTEEN-YEAR-OLD GRANDMOTHERS

When I was sixteen years old, little boys always wanted to be around me. Even back then, I knew that I was something special. I considered myself Mount Everest. Do you know how many men have died trying to get to the top of Mount Everest? After a while, they left me alone.

Now, I'm not saying no one's ever gotten on top of Mount Everest. Not all men die going to the summit. There are a select few that have made it and been conquerors. So just know that a few people have planted flags on Mount Everest — but that was a long time ago.

Today, sixteen-year-old girls are on the way to becoming grandmothers. These kids are fast. They grow up fast. I saw this one sixteen-year-old, she looked like she was getting ready for retirement. She had been used so much — it was sad. Back in my day, it was simple — you respected your elders and everybody. But most of all, you respected yourself — especially at that age, you had to act like a lady. These children, especially the ones that I see — pardon me, if you're not black and you're reading this — I'm talking about the people I see in my neighborhood — cussing and screaming and yelling, talking louder than the boys, wanting to fight. I'd never in my life seen little girls act like this.

I don't even know how to pronounce sixteen-year-old girls' names anymore. Where the hell are these names coming from? Lequisha and Aquanisha and Bonequida and Chaniqua. What the hell does all of that mean? Did somebody go back to Africa and find all these names under a bush? One girl's name was Vaginisha. I wonder what the hell was her mother thinking when she named her child Vaginisha.

Please, parents and parents-to-be, give your child a name that's respectable — that people will understand and not sit around trying to figure out even how to pronounce it. So when they go for a job interview, the employer will know how to say their name. Do you know by naming your child these crazy names, you automatically give them a disadvantage? Imagine your child going to interview at a Fortune 500 company. The secretary comes out and says, "Marisa Jones, you're next. Ms. Stacey Evans, you're next." And then she says, "Aquanisha Laquita Brown, you're next." I don't want my doctor named Vaginisha, unless it's a gynecologist. Do you really want your little girl to have to grow up and become a *gynecologist* just to get some respect?

I got a little bit off track. But these children are really, really moving way, way too fast. And I don't blame them, looking at this world, what's on television, in the music and everything going on around them — you have to grow up fast. It's a sad day when children can't be children and enjoy themselves. I'm glad I was sixteen when I was sixteen, and not right now. These children have it hard. What we have to do as adults is at least show them some values — show them how beautiful they really are — show them who they really are from the inside out. Let them know that they have the power to do anything that they want — more than just getting pregnant and being a mother at seventeen, more than the prom, more than being Vaginisha.

So, to repeat myself for emphasis, sixteen-year-old girls — slow down! Take your time and enjoy your teen years. I know it's hard to do it if you walk down the street and you have to walk around drug dealers, drug addicts, and pimps. I was reading an article in the newspaper about a man who goes and recruits strippers at high schools. It's sad. Having to deal with that and fight your way through the projects, fight your way to school, go through metal detectors, you have to grow up fast.

But, you sixteen-year-old girls, if I can leave you with something, if you will listen to me, here's what it is: Even though you're going through all that stuff, remember who you are and the power you have from within to be whoever you want to be. I'm glad that a lot of sixteen-year-old girls seem to like me and can listen to what I'm saying. So take your time. Make your mistakes but don't do nothing that's going to cost you your life! AIDS don't have no name on it. So the best kind of sex to have is none. But if you must — and I'm not condoning having sex — use a condom.

Let me repeat the example of our old

friend, the Frisbee. If you have a new Frisbee and you throw it out on the beach and a dog catches it — and then another dog catches it, and another. Pretty soon, that Frisbee is going to be all tow up — it ain't going to fly no more. So keep your Frisbee fresh and new by not throwing it to too many dogs. Like I said before, I ain't never met a man who says that he's looking for a nice ho to settle down with. Slow the hell down.

STAY IN SCHOOL

I wish I had done better in school. I didn't do that well in school because I was always in arguments with the teachers. We just didn't get along. My best subject was P.E. "Play and eat," that's what it stands for. I went every day for P.E., lunch, and recess. I got an A in P.E. and a B$^+$ in recess.

But on a serious note, school is very important. There are some children who are going to be all right no matter what. I see all these little boys playing basketball. They want to be NBA stars — they've got these hoop dreams and think that's one of the only ways out of the ghetto. Ain't nothing wrong with that if you've got the gift. That's what I say. If you can play basketball, be the best basketball player you can be. Play until your heart is content. But you also have to get an education. Remember, playing ball, you can get hurt. Something can go wrong. And everybody who goes out for the NBA don't even make it. Sometimes they make the NBP, which is the National Basketball Projects Association — only playing outside in the projects. So learn something, so you always have something to fall back on.

Then, there are the other ones who don't want to go to school because they're looking at the drug dealers selling dope. You see, sad to say, they don't always have anybody else to look up to in the 'hood. So they say, "If I can't be an NBA star, I'll just sell some dope." Selling dope is going to lead you to one of two places — to jail or to the grave — and I wouldn't recommend either place. But even if you still want to be a dope dealer, I still say *stay in school.* Learn how to count. That way, when the judge says he's giving you eighteen years, you'll be able to count backward from the day you go in. But I would ask that you put the calendar up high, so you don't have to bend over to see it.

Stay in school. Whatever you're going to do in life — if you're going to be a rapper, a basketball player — I wouldn't recommend you going out and being a dope dealer — doctors, lawyers, accountants, you're going to need an education. Even if you're going to work at McDonald's, you need to be able to count the change. I know a lot of people who ended up in horrible places because they never learned to read, write, and count. I know some successful people in the entertainment business who are broke because they got ripped off. People stole every dime off them because they didn't know how to read a contract and count. Learn something.

I've got to say this before I shut this chapter down. Selling that dope — listen. If you're the kind of person that wants to look over your shoulder for the rest of your life and you like that fast money, then go right ahead. But I'm going to tell you something. That fast money leaves faster than you make it. Looking over your shoulder every time you go to the bathroom is crazy as hell. Who wants that kind of stress! Even if you're a dope dealer, hell, you have an incentive to stay in school. You'll be able to count your own money. If you go to jail, it can still be an advantage — you'll be smarter than the rest of the prisoners there.

WHAT IN HELL IS "ACTING WHITE" SUPPOSED TO MEAN?

When kids in the 'hood do well in school, speak proper English, and get a good job, some people in the neighborhood say that these kids are "acting white" and turning their backs on them. I've got something to say to all those people, three little words: "Go . . . to . . . hell!" If speaking the king's English, getting a good job, and being able to afford what you want and have the American dream is acting white, then be white. It's the craziest thing I've ever heard. It's not acting white. It's acting like you've got some sense!

I get so sick of meeting the people who say this.

When I meet these same people I can't understand a thing they're saying. They can't even conjugate a verb. They don't know what a conjunction is. It's horrible. I stood at a counter at McDonald's for forty-five minutes trying to figure out what the lady was saying to me. She was saying, "May I take your order?" All I heard was "olba." "Ma . . . wha . . . te . . . olba."

Now, we have more positive role models who are intelligent black people. I remember they even said it about Oprah that she was acting white because she was speaking well and talking to white people. They said the same thing when Whitney Houston was singing all those pop ballads.

Oh, please! Get off this white-black thing,

just be! Education is a good thing no matter who you are. Bill and Camille Cosby and Barack Obama — they've made us proud. So now it's acceptable to speak proper English and wear nice suits. (How did looking like you're in prison get to be such a fashion statement?) So what we used to think was "white" is changing. It's not trying to be white anymore. It's being smart. Knowing your potential. Being a good representative of your family, your community, and the race of people you come from.

What I love about growing old and seeing this life change is knowing that we are opening up our minds to being an educated people. The 'hood is the 'hood, we love it and respect it, we thank God that we come from it — but you can't let the 'hood hold you back from your life and your education.

Back in the day, especially in the '70s, when this whole nonsense about acting white started happening — all the images we had were these black exploitation films. People jumping around on TV, acting silly, calling people honkies. What it did was say, If you don't act like this, you're acting white. That's all we had back then. But now the great thing is that we have a lot of people who represent us well. They show us that black people as a race are a lot of different

103

things. That's what's great about being black — we cover a huge range of who we are — from intelligent and well-spoken people to idiots standing on the corner.

The great thing about education and "acting white" (we're going to substitute "speaking well" from now on) — and coming where we come from — you can sit on the corner and shoot the breeze with Joe and talk about nothing — or you can sit at the president's table and talk to him about when he's leaving office. So it's better to have it and not need it than to need it and not have it.

WAKE UP! YOUNG PEOPLE, WAKE UP!

So with all of that said about education in the previous chapters, it's time to get our young people to wake up! What I've found about it is that there are some folks you can talk to until you're blue in the face — they're never going to get it and they're never going to change. But every once in a while, you'll run into someone who is eager to listen, eager to learn, and willing to try new things. Those are the people we need to reach. We have a responsibility as parents, older people, teachers, people in the neighborhood to recognize that.

If you see somebody with that spark in the

eyes who wants to be something more than where he or she comes from, it's up to us to cultivate that and reach out and help. Just like we see that positive spark in that person's eyes, so do all the negative people see that spark — and they want to destroy it and take it from the child. It's up to us to protect them. So how do we do that?

Okay. Here's a way to do it. If I see a man in the water in the ocean and a shark comes and bites both his legs off and he comes rolling back up on the sand, he doesn't have to tell me, "Don't go get into the water." I can sit there and look at his experience and know that I don't want to go through what he went through. It's the same thing with our young people. If we show them our experiences, what we had to go through and show them there's a better way — I'm only talking about these kids with the spark, you all know who I'm talking about — it can truly help them to find their way. The great thing about history is that if you learn from it, you're destined not to repeat the same thing. So all we can do to help people is to support and encourage them to try to be better.

I ain't going to talk to you until I'm blue in the face trying to make you change. I'm going to tell you what's on my mind and hope you get it and I'm going to move on.

That's what we have to do sometimes — move on. Try to help others, extend your hand, and then help the next. If they don't want to accept it, keep moving on. Don't let them discourage you. Never stop doing what you're doing because of somebody else's unwillingness to learn.

A lot of folks won't respect your wisdom. When you impart wisdom — whether they receive it or not — you've done your part. Even if it's your child — I know it's hard, but you give them all you can and then you have to move on because there's somebody else waiting for what you have to say.

The great thing about reaching out to help somebody is you know within yourself that you tried to help them and pass along all that you could. Whether they take it or not, your conscience is clear. You have a responsibility to make sure that the information you have is passed on.

This Hip-Hop Music

Hip-hop music is something that's very interesting. I like it — *some of it.* There are some really, really talented people coming up in this hip-hop music. But the sad thing is what it is we're going to be left with in twenty or thirty years.

What I don't like today is when they're

calling people "bitches and hos" and using "nigger" all the time. Those songs I don't want to listen to. I heard Usher sing a song about burning. If it's burning, Usher, you needs to get yourself to the clinic. Let's not talk about those lyrics. It's sad because all these kids know how to do today is cuss. It's crazy. I heard another song: "It gets no penetration if it smells like sanitation." What the hell kind of lyric is that in a song? I sat there thinking what kind of woman is going to sit there and listen to a man talking to her like that?

Take me back to real music. Music that made sense, lyrics that made you *feel* something. We had what they called "jump music." It was music that was so good that if you were going through something and you were depressed, you couldn't turn it on because it would make you jump off a bridge. Luther Vandross, Teddy Pendergrass, Linny Williams — those were all jump singers. You never turned on those songs if you were having relationship problems.

Take me back to lyrics that made sense. You know, "Close the door . . . let me give you what you've been waiting for. . . ." Music with mystery — ain't talking about no booty and sanitation. It just drives me up a wall, because I see these kids listening to it. Then these young ones who don't know their ABCs can recite words to these songs. If you're a musician, you have a certain amount of power as an artist and you have to be responsible for what you're putting out there. If you've got the power to teach all these kids and have all of them going in your direction listening to your music, then you ought to be saying something they can use.

Hell, if you really want to mess them up, give them an algebra equation or something in your songs. You want to rap, let's see you do that. Let's talk about some history. Let's talk about some black folk who meant something and changed the world — let them recite that. So when they get a test, they'll know what the answer is. But nobody wants to do that. They just want to talk about "this bitch," "this ho," "this is your momma and your daddy," and "where your booty is," and "flip your gun," and all that foolishness. It's crazy. What's wrong with these children?

Before we close this off, let me underline this for you because it's important. I can't stand folks going around with "nigger this," "nigger that," "nigger this," "nigger that." I have folks coming up to me talking like that and I'm sitting there thinking they've lost their minds. "Who the hell you talking to?" They say, "It's accepted within the culture."

It's on the radio — don't know how to conjugate a verb, and every other word out the mouth is "nigger," but you want somebody to take you seriously.

■ ■ ■ ■

PART FIVE
BEAUTY TIPS THAT
REALLY WORK

(MADEA TESTED AND APPROVED)

■ ■ ■ ■

Beauty is so important in our culture, so I thought it was important to let people know that you are beautiful no matter what size you are. Just because they make these tiny clothes for these models don't mean you ain't beautiful. Just look at me. As Oprah might say, "Accentuate the positive, even if you have to look hard to find it." Take out your little compact mirror that you use to powder your nose. Find something beautiful on your body and shine the mirror on it. It's a start.

THE MIRACLE OF VASELINE

Vaseline. I could write a book just on Vaseline alone. After you read this, you will understand why it is essential to keep some Vaseline on you at all times.

Vaseline is a miracle. Vaseline Petroleum Jelly was created by God for black people. People waste all that money on all that stuff to tighten their skin and firm it, lift it and separate it. All you need is some Vaseline. Stretch marks? Vaseline! Overweight? Vaseline! Pregnant? Vaseline! If you use Vaseline when you're pregnant, you won't get stretch marks and the baby will slip right out.

When people find out the history and how important Vaseline is, it will be dumb not to own some. Go out and stock up on Vaseline before the world's oil supply dries up. But buy the little jars, not the big ones. It takes too long to use them, and it's not so practical, since you must carry Vaseline in your purse at all times so you're ready for any situation that comes up.

I don't have no problem with chafing because of Vaseline. It's especially important when you put on a pair of stockings, Big Mommas — those are the kind that I wear. You put on those Big Momma stockings and you start walking down the street. You have to put on some Vaseline on the inner part of your thighs before putting those stockings on. There's even a warning label on the stockings — it says, "Note: Warning. Please, Vaseline the inner part of your thighs before you put on these stockings. If not, fires have started. It will melt your Frisbee."

There ain't nothing worse than barbecued stuff. Smoke will be coming from between your legs. The fire department will come out in full force, like they're trying to put out a burning bush fire. So please Vaseline before, especially if you're a woman my size. You have to be careful. If you put some of that Vaseline on, not only will you get the nice, smooth walk, there will be no need for anybody to call 911.

Vaseline is the cure for anything you got going on. Did you know that? If you boil some Vaseline and put it in some water and drink a little teaspoon of it, it'll cure the common cold. People don't know that. Well, that's what people tell me — I ain't never tried it. Hell, I ain't that crazy.

Black people don't buy ChapStick because it's too expensive. One jar of Vaseline can last you four winters for a family of twenty. You put it on your lips when they get rough. Beauty queens have used it for years so they can smile for hours without their lips sticking to their teeth.

Another thing — black people, when they get out of the tub, we get what we call "ashy." If you're not black, you don't understand this, but if you are, you can relate. If you get out of the tub and you don't start to moisturize with Vaseline right away, it starts to happen to you immediately. It starts at your feet. You begin to turn white. You have to be careful, because if you live in the ghetto and you walk out of your house ashy you are in for trouble. They will think you are a white person coming out of somebody's house, and there can be trouble. This is the honest-to-God truth. Not only does your skin turn another shade of white, it dries out completely. The darker they are, the more ashy they get. You could use all sorts of moisturizers. But what I found out is really simple: Vaseline is cheapest and works best. So if you ever see somebody ashy walking by, just remind them, Vaseline! (Now, if you are an actual white person and you're in the ghetto and you run into some trouble, this should give you an idea: You can tell people you ran out of Vaseline and you're ashy and you're running — and you should be running — to the store to get some more. As previously mentioned, don't try to show off any dance moves, or they will figure you out for sure.)

I use it in my hair, under my makeup, I use it under my arms when I don't have deodorant. It's also a really good butt softener. As I said before, it also gets rid of stretch marks after a baby. You just have to apply it twenty-two times a day.

Back in the day, I used to have to carry in my handbag all the woman's stuff, but you know those days are over for me. I've been through the change, so I don't have to carry all that stuff. I just carry the fan now because I have my "personal summers" where I just get really hot but that's about it. I've got my pistol in there. (You know you can use Vaseline to grease your pistol, too. That's right. It makes your bullets smooth, and they can't run a ballistics test to trace it back to your gun.)

I use Vaseline for everything. I don't even use oil in my car. I use, you guessed it, Vaseline! If my seats are dried and chapped in my car, I don't buy Armor All and spend all that money. I use Vaseline. Do you know that after you wash your car and you want the tires to shine, don't go out and spend nothing on those tire-shiners. Get you some Vaseline. It'll last longer. Car wax, hell, no. Vaseline.

You don't need Binaca. Just a little bit of Vaseline under your tongue can change the whole way your breath smells. It will make it smooth, that's right. With Vaseline, you'll never need mouthwash. As a matter of fact, I don't use toothpaste. Give me some Vaseline and baking soda. Makes your teeth shine like money and your breath smell great.

BE NATURAL

Have you ever been to a pool party where a whole bunch of black women are standing around looking cute? At the pool, they put their feet in and their legs in, but not their heads. Then, if they get into the water, their hair will never get wet. Now, I understand that. Of course, you want to look your best. Black women ain't going to get their hair done and then have to go right back to the hairdresser. It ain't like a white woman, who can just wash it and get up and shake it and go on out the door. No, it takes preparation and chemicals and glue and saturation and hours and hours to get that hair to lay down and look like it does. There ain't nothing wrong with it. I'm proud of it if that's what you want to do.

But what I don't understand is this hair-weave thing. They take this strip of hair from a horse or something and put it in the head. They glue it and they try to blend in their real hair with the horse hair. Nine times out of ten, their hair is rougher and more coarse than the horse hair they done put in. So what you get is a really rough spot at the top, and the further down it goes, the longer and the smoother it gets. Now that's crazy as hell.

My thing is "be natural." If you want to get it permed, go get it permed. If it's hair that's an inch off your head and you want to perm it, perm it. But it's something else when you go and put all that other stuff on. Everybody's going to know good and well that you didn't grow no hair that looks like that. I saw Beyoncé; she looked like something out of *The Lion King,* she had so much hair coming out of her head. What the hell, be natural. There ain't nothing wrong with it. Be who you is. That's right, who you is! If your hair don't grow but a half inch, then wear it. If it grows down your back, then let it be that. But don't try to be something you're not. Let your hair be what it is.

THE MYSTERY OF THE BLOND-HAIRED, BLUE-EYED BLACK WOMEN

Let's talk about wigs. If you want to wear a wig and it makes you look nice, then that's fine. A lot of people need to wear wigs. That's all great as long as you ain't four shades darker than the blond wig on your head. I saw a woman with a blond wig and blue contacts in her eyes, and she was darker than Kunta Kinte. Who is she trying to be? That's crazy as hell. It don't even look right. It makes me just want to walk up to them and just slap them and say, "What the hell, wake up!"

Don't they know the blond look went out in the 1970s, when black women were trying to be white. The only reason why black women were trying to be white before then was that's all they used to see on TV was white women. The only black women you saw were mammy or the maid. They weren't pretty and nobody wanted to be like them.

Nowadays, black women are enjoying being black. Catch up! Be proud of your black skin. Black don't crack! If you take care of it, you'll be in your forties and fifties and still look like you're twenty. Take a look at me. Take a look at the cover of this book and look at that picture. I'm sixty-eight and I know I look good. I ain't never had no blond wig and blue eyes. I'm who I am. I just use Vaseline.

THE CURSE OF THE JHERI CURL

When a white man begins to go bald, they freak out. They call the Hair Club for Men. I understand that, but let nature take its course, because those comb-overs look like hell. But I don't blame them for trying, because they don't necessarily look right without their hair. Some of these white men get that kind of skinhead look.

But black men in that situation, they just say, "Oh well," and they cut it all off. When the hairline starts to go back and it's looking funny, they just shave it all off and they walk around bald. I like that. I love a man with a bald head. You look at most of these people walking around like that, most of them have bald spots. Michael Jordan's got a bald spot. He said, "The hell with it. I'll shave it off."

I don't think it's the hair that is sexy. It ain't about the hair. It's about the back of the neck. If you can grip the back of the neck and it fits your hand, then look out! That's sexy. Some of you know what I'm talking about.

Some men ain't going bald but they have what we call "waves." They wear these do-rags. The problem I have with do-rags is that they have the audacity to wear them out in public. I'm so sick of seeing these do-rags. It's today's version of that plastic bag that men and women had with the Jheri curls. You know that plastic bag? There would be steam coming off the top of their heads when they'd take it off. They'd be walking around in public with that thing on. Take that off your damned head!

Speaking of plastic bags, let's talk about the Jheri curl for a minute. I've lived through all kinds of devastation in my life. I've lived through a man who had a perm in the '50s, Afros in the '70s, and Jheri curls in the '80s. Hazardous! Just like asbestos is killing a whole bunch of people — and they just found this out — you just wait until they find out the effects of the Jheri curl.

I remember my second husband, or maybe it was my fourth (I get them all confused because they all were worth the same amount of insurance — that's how I remember them). This one had just got his Jheri curl. I don't know if you know this, but when you first get your hair done, the smell of the chemicals would just be horrible. I couldn't sleep with him. I kicked him out of the bed one night. It smelled so bad that I kicked him all across the room. It just had this foul odor, and you carry it on you for seven days.

When we were walking down the street one day, buzzards were flying over his head, and I knew something had to be wrong with this picture.

Don't get me started. Jheri curls were a mess — and the damned thing was flammable. I don't know who the hell invented it, but I wish I could find Mr. Jheri. I'd sue the hell out of him. I had to get new slipcovers for my couch because I got stains all over it from the Jheri curls.

Let me tell you something — people who made pillows got rich. He made Sealy Posturepedic rich because we had to buy new mattresses all the time. That's what happened to a friend of mine. He had a Jheri curl, and he went to bed, and he was smoking. He got up to go to the bathroom and laid the cigarette down by the bed — the bed caught on fire because it's flammable from all the Jheri-curl chemicals — burned his whole apartment, burned the whole apartment down. Everybody in there had Jheri curls. So, one mattress led to the other. They had to call in the haz-mat people because of the chemicals — it was like a train derailment. They had to bring in all these different specialists to come in and get all these chemicals out of the air. That's what happened to the hole in the ozone layer. Them damned

Jheri curls. Now that the Jehri curl is over, the people who hug the trees are much happier. It's no longer around, so the ozone can heal.

I'm so glad the Jheri curl is over. You know, Jerry Lewis did Jerry's Kids. I was going to do the Jheri Curl Kids and have a telethon to raise money to get help. That's what's wrong with these children, too — it's the Jheri curl. Those chemicals seeped through their scalp, went down to the placenta. People who put them chemicals in their hair and had babies! All those kids are crazy as hell. You've heard of the baby boomers? Well, now we've got the Jheri boomers.

BURN THE BRA

I don't believe in them. I never did. What happens is, they pick you up and make you look nice and everything. But back in my day, the ones they had made you look like you had two torpedoes heading straight for Cuba. If I lifted my stuff up and put it out there, I could set a table on it and prepare Thanksgiving dinner in the presence of mine enemies, right on the top of my brassiere.

I just like to go free. Let them go where they will. If they fall, let them fall. If they go up, let them go up. If they want to lay down when I lie on my back, they can run down my side. It's okay. It's about freedom. It's about freedom of choice. If the left one wants to go to the right and the right one wants to go to the left, or if I just take both of them and throw them over my shoulder, it's all right.

I'm with whoever burned the bra. Angie Dickerson, was it? Angela Davis? I don't know who it was, somebody named Angela who burned the bra. Thank you for burning that bra. And if you want to warm up all of Kuwait this winter, you can burn mine.

THE UNNATURAL LOOK

I saw a woman — she had fingernails that were about twenty inches long. I was wondering — she walked up to me and wanted to shake my hand. I said, "Hell no. I don't know how you wipe nothing with that. How do you wash your hands?" You know, all the diamonds and everything else she had on it. It had her name spelled out. Her husband's name. And a boyfriend. By the way, this is the same woman who had the blond wig and blue contacts in her eyes. I wish I had a picture of her so you could see her, but you already know what she looked like. She looked like something out of the circus.

It made me think back about all these different cultures in *National Geographic* that have all these different rituals and things. I don't know where all these long fingernails come from. It must be the culture of the ghetto. That looks crazy as hell.

You know what also looks unnatural? Plastic surgery. I've been in California a lot lately, and they done pulled their eyes and head back so far that their lips are back on the side of their faces. For years, black folk had big lips, full lips. In the community, it was a terrible thing. They'd talk about each other — "Oh, them lips so big, lips so big" and "I want little thin lips." That all goes back to watching white women on television.

Now all these folks are trying to get big lips, trying to make their lips fat and full. Those poor celebrities like Michael Jackson who went out and got his lips trimmed and slimmed! I know he must be pissed as hell.

If you are thinking about plastic surgery, let's stop right here and have a little talk first. Let me tell you something — every line, every bag, every wrinkle, every pound you put on means you done learned something on this earth. You need to embrace it. You ain't supposed to be beautiful all your life. You ain't supposed to stay the same. Your breast and your butt are supposed to sag. As I told you before: we came from dirt, and the reason everything is sagging is because that dirt is pulling you back to where you came from. That's where you're going to have to go when you die. Stop trying to slow it down — let it happen naturally.

Now, I do understand there are some folks that plastic surgery helps. And they need it — my God, do they need it! So, in that case, I say, "Baby, go ahead and do it. Can I give you a little money from this Jheri-curl telethon to help you get some plastic surgery?" But most of the time, I say again, "Black don't crack," so you don't need it as much. Let it be. Be natural as much as you can. Enjoy your life. Enjoy being older. The more you fight getting older, the worse it's going to be for you. But if you learn how to embrace it and embrace yourself and who you are, to hell with what people think.

Be the best you can be. If you think you're fat and you don't like it, change it. If you like being fat and it don't bother you, that's okay with me. Honestly, if you wake up in the morning and look at yourself and you think you're fine, then the hell with everybody. But if you're really miserable, then I say, go ahead and change it.

I ain't no fan of none of this other stuff that will make you look better without you learning how to feel better on the inside first. Take care of what's wrong on the inside first. Then, if you still need to do that stuff, go ahead and do it. So my thing is, whatever you don't like, change it, but change it from the inside first.

■ ■ ■ ■

PART SIX
DON'T ASK DR. MADEA

■ ■ ■ ■

ADVISORY
The advice contained in this chapter may be
hazardous to your health or kill you.

THE FRIED-EVERYTHING DIET

Back in the day, I would be considered what was called "fine." A good thirty, forty years ago, I would be considered sexy. Just go back and look at some old pictures of real people, like Marilyn Monroe and Pearl Bailey, Aretha Franklin. You go back and look at them. You will see how it was to be sexy way back then.

Nowadays, you look at the magazines, and all you see are these skinny girls everywhere. I don't understand it. There's nothing sexy about a rib cage. Men don't want no rib cage, what the hell! Back in my day, men wanted some meat on the bone. So that's why I eat to stay fine. You look at little Beyoncé. She's got an old woman's booty but the rest of her body is a little too skinny, so that ain't sexy. Sexy was when you are even all over. You are 45-40-45. That's sexy.

I eat because I got to stay this size because I want to keep a man. See, when you're full-figured like I am, it's easy to keep a man, especially in the winter. In the summertime, they don't want to be around you because you're too hot all the time. And to tell you the truth, I don't want to be around them, either. But in the wintertime, they'll snuggle up against you to stay warm, especially if you ain't paid the gas bill. This is particularly true if you got a skinny man — believe me, he's really going to be up under you.

My favorite food is fried. Period. Whatever's fried, that's my favorite. The deeper you fry it . . . the better. I love fried everything: fried chicken, fried catfish, fried potatoes, fried collard greens.

My diet is "Eat till you're full, drink till you fall out, and then get up the next day and do it again." Now, I can do that for as long as I live. (I am a diabetical right now, so I have to slow down some. You know, you can't eat everything when you're a diabetical. They tell me it's because of my diet. But I don't know, because I have a cousin named Eileen. She used to eat a whole lot of food, too. She got it, too, but she was real skinny. So I don't know what they're saying. All I know is somebody's making some money on this insulin they selling. They're selling insulin like dope. More folk got diabetes these days than ever before. What happened? Back in the day, you never heard about diabetes. Now everybody's got it. I don't know. Something must be in the water.)

One day they tell you that you can eat something, then the next day, they tell you it's unhealthy. I don't understand all these people say they're experts. Expert in this! Expert in that! How the hell are you an expert in food! Yeah, I'm an expert in food — fried food!

I don't understand why they say that if you stop eating this, you're going to lose weight. I've been on every diet there was. This one time I was trying to get into this pair of jeans that I had bought . . . I bought them hot — if you don't know what that means, it's means somebody is selling them on the corner and you buy them. They were really, really expensive. They weren't my size, but I wasn't going to pass up a good deal. So I was trying to lose some weight, get these pants on, and somebody said, "Don't eat no carbs." What the hell is a carb? And somebody else said don't eat too many calories. I don't got time to sit around and count this calorie and that calorie . . . I'm just going to eat and do what I got to do.

All I know is when I'm hungry, I'm going

to eat. When I'm dead, I'll stop eating. Something is going to take me out of here, if it's a stroke or however it comes, I'm going to eat and die happy. All these people around here trying to be healthy, you can go out there and get hit by a bus tomorrow and be ninety-two pounds. Then, you're going to think, "Damn, I should have ate that cake!"

If I got down to ninety-eight pounds and had a nice little figure like some of these girls and got hit by a bus, I'd be so pissed that I did all that dieting. Hit by a train tomorrow and wasted all your life trying to eat right and you're dead. Oh, girl, you know what they'll say when you're dead. "Girl, she sure looks good in that casket, ain't she thin. Look at her waist." To hell with that, I'm going to eat me some cake. Every day I wake up. I eat whatever the hell I want to eat. I'm happy. So if I die of anything, it's because I was eating happy. Hell, put me in a closed casket if it bothers you so much.

To be honest, I do feel kind of bad in the morning. I got to roll out of the bed, sit up for about twenty minutes, then stand up on one leg and get it ready to go, then stand up on the other leg, get the circulation going. Then I try to take a shower. Stand up under some hot water to get the circulation in my head. Get my blood pressure down because my head would be spinning. I don't know what that's from. Somebody tried to tell me it's from all the fried food, but I don't believe it.

And one last very important thing about fried food: swelling. Sometimes my spirit tells me that I'm about to get arrested. That's right, arrested. So what I do is eat a lot of fried stuff, more than usual, and the fluid would build up in me. This last time I had this fluid, my ankles were swollen real big and I got arrested. God is good. You see, what happened, they put me under house arrest. I stopped eating all the fried foods, and the fluid went down. I slipped the house arrest bracelet right off my foot, and I was ready to go on and do whatever I needed to do. Find me something fried! I went straight to get me some chicken.

FIT FOR WHAT?

To me, fitness means that if you wake up in the morning and you open your eyes, then you're fit. If you can move, you're fit. Fit to do what, the hell if I know. You might not be fit to make it to the kitchen or to fit into those jeans, but you're fit if you can open your eyes. My personal fitness test is "Can I make it to the car to get to Dunkin' Donuts to get me a doughnut today?" If I do that,

I'm all right. I exercise, though — I exercise my left and right arm picking up the fork and the knife to eat.

I also get me a nice workout going from the car to the grocery store to the fried chicken section to pick up something to bring back to the house. I also exercise going from the door to the mailbox to check the mail. I'm always looking for a check, or to see what checks have bounced.

There's another way you get fit: running like hell from the police. Who the hell needs a treadmill? Drive down my street late at night, get pulled over, the po-po pull out their billy clubs, and you run like hell. That's good exercise.

GLAUCOMA MEDICINE

I've had glaucoma since I was fifteen. I know you may be thinking this was a little early, that it usually comes a little later on. But the doctor told me. My doctor was not only a regular doctor but he was a futuristic doctor. He told me, "If you take this, in the future you will have no glaucoma." And I could see clear.

Don't follow my example. Live your own life. My example works for me. You see, everybody's got to find what works for them. If I didn't have glaucoma, I wouldn't take the medicine. Do you understand what I'm trying to tell you? Because I have glaucoma, I have to roll it up . . . I mean I have to take the medicine and it helps me see. Then it makes me hungry . . . which messes up my diet. So it goes all around in circles. You have to make a choice; either you'll be able to see or you're skinny.

You have to roll the glaucoma medicine from the left to the right if it's your left eye that has the glaucoma. If it's the right eye with the glaucoma, you roll from the right to the left. You have to sprinkle and lick and roll. Sprinkle. Lick. Roll. Kind of like . . . I better stop here. I don't want no parental advisory on the cover of this book.

Nobody should be following what I'm saying unless you got glaucoma the same way I got it. I've got a special case of glaucoma that's very rare — it's only eligible for a few people to get this prescription, and I don't think it's you. Because you ain't me. Your doctor . . . my doctor stands on the corner of Twenty-Ninth and Third and passes out his prescriptions, and you have to buy a dime of it. If your doctor is my doctor, then you might have the same thing. But if you don't know my doctor, please leave the glaucoma drugs alone. As I said, it's a very special prescription.

I don't have to hide my glaucoma medicine. I just thank God that I'm a woman of means, which means I can mean to hide anything anywhere I want to. I have folds and creases under folds and crevices that I didn't even know were there. You got to follow stretch mark A to get to crease number C to get to fold number D, which will lead you to the glaucoma medicine, which will help you with your eyes. If you're looking for a roadmap to heaven, follow these stretch marks along my thighs!

The young people don't necessarily know that I am on glaucoma medicine. You see, glaucoma medicine is from the earth. It's pure. This ain't drugs. It's been around since Native Americans (what we used to call "Indians") with the peace pipe. That's why all of them could see so good to shoot those arrows. Nowadays, I use a pistol. If my aim is going to be right, I have to make sure my eyes are right. You never know when a man is going to drive you up a wall.

Drugs are a serious thing. They say if you can say you can stop anytime, then you don't have a problem. See, I'm the kind of person that can stop it at any time if it is taking too much of me or overtaking me. Not that I've ever actually tried to stop — for fear of endangering my vision, of course.

I know my personality. I think if your momma was a drunk, your daddy was a drunk, everybody in your family was a drunk, and that's what you grew up with and you've been drinking since you were two, you might need to take a look at yourself. If you're the type of person that picks up a drink every four or five months on a special occasion and you don't get tow down (where you can't see or stand up), you might be all right. That's me. I'm *in control!*

The minute you get out of control, and you're walking around in the middle of the night banging on people's doors and asking them for favors. Like my granddaughter, who came by the house banging on the door talking about she was hungry at four o'clock in the morning. I threw some food out the window to her because I wasn't getting up out of my bed. (I keep me a plate of chicken beside the bed in case I get hungry in the middle of the night. That way, I don't have to go down to the refrigerator.) See, she's addicted to that stuff and it's bad, because she had a baby out there with her at four o'-clock in the morning in a book bag. It wasn't a baby backpack that she put the child in, but a book bag with Barney on it that she had cut the legs out of and put the child's legs hanging out of the holes. So I fed her, but that's terrible.

Remember: glaucoma medicine is only supposed to enhance your eyes. If glaucoma medicine is making you want to walk around in your birthday suit when you know that you're supposed to have a suit covering your birthday suit, you've had too much.

I say all of this to say, leave drugs and alcohol alone. Don't mess around with the stuff because it all leads to something. Now, they told me this glaucoma medicine was going to lead to something, but all it led to was my seeing.

ADDICTED TO NICOTINE

I think I started smoking at six. They say that secondhand smoking is just the same as smoking, so maybe I started smoking in the womb. My mother smoked and drank all the way up to the time I was born. She'd take a drink and push, take a drink and push, take a drink and push. See, they didn't have epidurals or anesthesia back then. They used to give you Jack Daniel's and Hennessy. That's cognac. You drink it and have a baby all the while you're laughing.

Yeah, I've been smoking for a very, very long time. The doctor told me that I have to quit because my lungs look like Bill Duke. I used to steal cigarettes from my uncles because my mother didn't like me smoking. The house was full of smoke, like a club.

Smoking cigarettes made me feel as glamorous as all the white women in *Life* magazine, because they all had a cigarette back then. It made me feel sexy when I was in my teens. You know, I was smoking on the pole. I was smoking when I was pregnant, too. There weren't nobody telling you back then to stop. You was smoking and drinking all the way until the baby came. Then you wonder why the baby looked the way it did.

You know, it's addicting. They didn't tell me that. Do the math. I've been smoking cigarettes for sixty-two years. It's that nicotine. I've tried to quit. Every time I try to quit, I gain forty-five pounds. I know it's not the fried foods, because I'm still eating the same twelve pieces a day. I don't understand where the weight is coming from. So when I got up to about 280, I said to hell with this. I just kept getting heavier and heavier.

But I know that I need to quit because it ain't no good for you. And it ain't no good for your bank account. I know that I have spent at least twenty-two million dollars on cigarettes. And for what — to get cancer? That's crazy as hell. I wish I could quit. If you know somebody who can help me, let me know.

Going to the Gynecologist and Other Medical Annoyances

Three places I don't want to go to: the gynecologist, the dentist, and Hell. All three seem to be exactly the same place.

A man once asked me what it was like to be examined by a gynecologist. I told him if anybody ever put these metal instruments down your throat and pulled your testicles up through your nose, that's what a vaginal exam feels like. That's the answer. That's the way I answer a silly question like that. He got real quiet. I wonder why.

But, ladies, you have to go and get your checkups. Please get your checkups. Get your mammogram. If something's going on, don't be scared to find out. Go in there and find out so you can face it. Do you know that I know people who will run and have plastic surgery done in a minute but will put off having a regular medical exam forever? What good is looking good if you ain't checked yourself out? If you think something's going on, it probably is. So the earlier you find out, the better it may be for you. Maybe I should listen to my own advice. See, I go every three or four years, which I know ain't enough.

Are you one of those folks who sees a sign and says, "I better go to the doctor, but I don't have time." Even if you're working hard day and night, make time, because your health is important. If you're like me, eating all these fried foods and smoking cigarettes, you might want to get yourself checked sooner than later. Your warranty may have expired.

So what I say, if it ain't broke, don't fix it. But if you feel it breaking, you go get it fixed. It's just like your car. If your oil light is coming on, you don't just put your finger over it and hide it. Take the car into the shop. Your body is a finely tuned machine. You've got to take care of it.

They caught my diabeticalness early, but then it was up to me to follow the rules. I was able to be on insulin pills . . . at first. But then they told me to stop eating and start exercising, and I didn't do that, so then I went on to the shots. Then, they told me, if I don't stop eating stuff, I'm going to lose my kidney and go on dialysis. We'll see what comes. But right now, I'm going to find me some cookies.

Hell, I know it's aggravating at the doctor's with all that digging and pushing and scraping and cutting. You know, the worst thing I hate to hear the doctor say is, "This is going to make you feel uncomfortable." He starts and his expression never changes, and you're about to jump up off the table. I kicked the hell out of one of them. From then on, he's been really careful when he comes close to me. He wears a cup.

There's another person I hate to go to — the dentist. People tell me they like my teeth. I say, thank you, I just got them made, because I could never go to the dentist. Oh, Lordy, it was so much pain. But I wish I would've kept my teeth, because then I'd be able to eat this chicken better. I have to chew it now on one side so the glue don't come loose on the dentures — make sure they all stay on tight.

Prevention? They told me I could have avoided all this stuff if I had eaten right and exercised. Oh, well. I'm here now and I've got to deal with it. But I always get three or four different opinions on whatever is going on. I make the time. If I got a cavity, I got to go to three or four different dentists, so I can find out what's going on. Not only that, you get to find the cheapest price to get it filled. Yes, I bargain-shop, even for the dentist.

These doctors will give you all kinds of prescriptions for everything. And these prescriptions are as expensive as hell. Do you know that I had to make a choice between paying my mortgage and buying my prescription? They were both nine hundred dollars. For some pills!

What happened to back in the day, when we had remedies for everything. When you didn't have no soap, do you know what we used to use? Lysol! Lysol will clean you better than soap. For rashes and stuff, my grandmother would take some ammonia, take a couple of capfuls and boil it and she'd put it in the tub. You'd sit there and take a bath in it. When you got up — I don't know if it worked or you didn't want to sit in the ammonia ever again — but you made that rash go away some kind of way.

There were certain roots and branches — she'd go out there and pick stuff up. I wish I had learned all this stuff she would do. She'd come in there and whatever was bothering you, you'd feel better. Even if you didn't want to take it no more and you psyched yourself up into feeling better or you just felt better. But they didn't pass none of that stuff down on me. The biggest remedy I got from her was this stuff called shellac. Shellac was a root, I don't know where it came from, but that was her name for it. It could be called something else. But she'd go out and boil it and put it in the food. What it would do is give you diarrhea and clean you out. You'd wake up feeling twenty pounds lighter. When you ate a whole buffet in fifteen minutes, that thing would make you really feel better.

There's another natural remedy that I know very well. It's called by many names, but my favorite is weed. The professional term: glaucoma medicine. I know it very well. I know it works. I know it relaxes, and it even saves lives. After I've had some glaucoma medicine, it kept me from killing my husband once or twice.

DEPRESSION

I told you earlier how depressed I got, starting the day that I got pregnant. My postpartum depression stayed with me for forty-eight years, until the day Cora left home. People around me didn't know how bad it was. I tried to hide it. It was my biggest secret. I love Cora to death, but it was tough raising her and not being able to work that pole no more. After I had her, everything dropped. I couldn't pull it up no more. That depressed me. Before Cora, my body was fine. I was a goddess. That's why they called me Delicious. I was mmm-mmm-good, like the soup. Now, when I look in the mirror, I just say, "Oh, well, mm, mm, mm, nasty."

So the only way out of it is find other things to be happy about. I would look at my daughter and just enjoy watching her have a good life. I'd love to hear her laugh. I'd love to see her eat. You know, at three she knew the number to Domino's and was ordering pizza — did I tell you that? All that stuff impressed me because she was a survivor. But I digress.

Depression is a very serious subject. Remember, I'm not a doctor, I'm not a professor, I'm not a psychologist. Hell, I didn't even graduate high school. So you take this advice at your own risk. If you're depressed, you probably sure in the hell ain't reading this book anyway, but maybe you should pass it along to somebody who is.

If you are depressed, there are a few things that you automatically do in your depression. You go find the darkest room in your house, you close the curtains, you put on some sad music, you don't want to talk to nobody, you take the phone off the hook.

Trust me, I've been there. In addition to getting pregnant with Cora, I've been there over bills, over men, over life, over family, just sitting up crying and crying and crying. But what I found out, the longer you sit there and feel bad about yourself, the longer you're going to stay depressed. You wonder why nobody cares, why nobody wants to be around you. Can I give you a tidbit of information, whether you want to hear it or not? The reason why nobody wants to be around you is because your ass is depressed. You bring them down when you come around.

If you want people to come around you, there are certain things you've got to do. You got to get up and fight your way through it. You know, the minute you get up and change your attitude about what's going on, the other stuff on the outside of you changes. If you're depressed about being fat, then, hell, lose the weight. Go to the gym. Do something. Even if you lose half a pound, it don't matter. At least you're making an effort to get better. Whatever is kicking you and trying to push you down, I say kick back. If you've got a purse like mine, pull your pistol out and shoot at it, unless it's a human being (you might get in trouble, get put in jail, and become even more depressed).

The first thing you do to get over your depression is open up the curtains, put on some good music, take you a shower, get up, put on a good face, and open the door and go out and see the world. Everything that's kicking you, kick it back. I'm a fighter. I like to fight.

You're sitting around waiting for your man to come fix it, your family and friends to come fix it, it ain't never going to happen. God can fix it, but it's got to be fixed through you. You can sit around praying all you want, "God help me, God help me." But God ain't going to do a thing until you get up and do something yourself. Everything starts with you. You have to start doing things yourself to change your life. When you put yourself in motion, then everybody around you gets moving, too. They wonder what's going on. God and people don't want to be helping anybody who doesn't want to be helping themselves.

The worst thing you can do is hold things in. See, you got to be real careful about that, especially in marriage or family matters. If something is bothering you, don't sit there and hold it. Say it. Tell them what's bothering you. They might think you're nagging and working on their nerves, but it's better you get it out than be holding on to all that stuff yourself.

Well, let me backtrack a little — you sometimes have to draw the line what you're talking about. Some things you let pass — you don't want to fight about everything. But something that's really bothering you that you can't straighten out, you say something about it. However you're feeling, you let it be known. Deal with that emotion, on that day, at that minute at that time. That way, things don't have a chance to build up and go crazy in you. That's what I have to do. I can't be sitting around holding all this stuff in, as crazy as I am, I'd be on a rampage. I would be insane. I'd go postal. I have to take it one kick-ass moment at a time.

GOOD TIMES

Please, enjoy every minute of the good times. Now, I know what you're thinking: Dr. Madea, that's not medical advice! But believe me, if we're going to talk about depression, we're sure as hell going to talk about the good times, too.

The good times don't come that often for most people. You know what, I hate it when people who have something good happening to them start to say, "Oohhh, everything's going too good, something bad is going to happen." I don't believe that. I think that if you keep putting out good, good has got to keep coming back to you.

Just as much of a struggle and pain you have going through the bad times, take that much laughter and joy in the good times. Enjoy every second of it. Take your time. We go through so much hell in this life, from husbands, children, cars that don't work, trying to obey laws and drive at the right speed limit. All of that is just hell for me, especially traffic. So we've got to learn how to enjoy the little things.

If you can get out into your car in the morning and go on the freeway and not be in traffic, you're having a good day. When things are going good, sit there, enjoy the moment, and take it all in. Don't be rushing through it, hurrying off to something else. No, "savor" is what they call it — that's a rich white-folk word. Take your time. Take your shoes off and walk barefoot through it. But put some Vaseline on your feet first. Feel everything. Smell everything. Taste everything.

Some people say that you're going to have as many bad days as you have good days on this earth. I don't necessarily agree with that. As I said before, I believe you can have more good days than bad if you *make* them a good day. I've had good days after good days after good days.

Like I remember this time I kept getting lucky, hitting the number 7, the Lucky 7 on the lottery. For three days, I just kept making money. Those were some of the best days of my life. God, it sure was good. I wish I could have about twenty more years like that of winning everything like that in a row. There was another time when I got off house arrest — that was a good time for me. Remember the time when that house arrest bracelet came off because I wasn't eating the fried foods? That was one of the best days of my life. See, when you're forced to be locked down and you get free, oh, that feels real good. When you get that freedom, you're all right! Simple pleasures can go a long way.

THE BEST MEDICINE

My momma used to tell me, stand for something or you'll fall for anything. You've got to take a stand, find what you can believe in and fight for in this life. What is your passion? My passion is fried food. I will fight like hell with anyone who tries to take my Crisco from me.

You know what I've found out about passion? It's your destiny. If you're trying to find your passion, all you got to do is keep getting up every day. It'll find you. Destiny has a way of creeping up on you. If you're depressed and struggling and frustrated and don't know what to do or what your purpose is on this earth, I have one suggestion for you: wake up every morning and thank God that you're doing it. Get out in the world. It will find you, and it will hit you so hard right between the eyes — when it's time.

Most important, you've got to have an open attitude and welcome it. Because if you ain't ready for it, you ain't never going to find it. Let's say you're supposed to be a great writer. If you're sitting around letting everything bother your nerves and you ain't never sat down to write your first word, you won't find your destiny. You've got to get yourself in a good place where you can sit down and clear your head and see what life is saying to you. It's a really subtle thing. If you walk through this life, it speaks to you every day and tells you which way to go. But if your life is so crowded and chaotic, you won't be able to hear it. Once you find it, it ain't going to let you go. It's going to find you. Just keep getting up every day.

My passion, besides fried food, is about helping people feel better about themselves — not letting people or this life walk over you or talk to you in any kind of way. I like to show people how to get up and get a life. Sometimes, I drag them kicking and screaming (especially the ones in my family), because you ain't going to sit in my house depressed and working on my nerves. You're going to get the hell out of there or I'm going to force you to get a life — or a death.

It's about being happy and laughing. You know, people just don't laugh no more. You got to laugh every day, and laugh hard. Laugh as hard as you work, that's my motto. I find humor in so much stuff. I can find humor in somebody walking down the street. I just sit there and look and start laughing.

Next time you're sitting in traffic, just look

at the people around you. I play this game called "let me put words in their mouth." So if you see somebody on the cell phone, make up what you think they're saying in your own head. If you come up with really funny things, it's a great form of entertainment. Do you ever catch people picking their noses at a red light? And you just sit there and stare at them and then they realize that you're looking. All that kind of stuff is nasty but it can be funny!

Just stop for a minute. Stop getting worked up and just start laughing at some of this stuff. The alternative, if you don't laugh at it, is it can really weigh you down and destroy you.

There are some things that happen on this earth that you ain't got no control over. The best thing you can do to make it easier to bear and get through it is to find a way to make it funny. I have seen some of the funniest funerals in my life. I know it's supposed to be a sad occasion, but I have seen things at funerals that made me fall over laughing. I was laughing so hard I had to bend over and act like I was crying.

Another thing I have no control over, even though I vote, I ain't got no control over this president. So I sit there and laugh at him at every chance I can get. He's hilarious.

MEN ALL PAUSE

There was a song by Klymaxx called "The Men All Pause." That's basically what I feel about menopause. You get to that point in your life, when you're through what we called back in the day "the change," and every man around you will pause. They'll pause and think about everything they're saying to you, before they say it, how they say it, when they're going to say it, and why they're going to say it. In short, they will question every bit of their masculinity before they talk or say something to you when they're going through this "pausing point."

Let me break this word down. Men-o-pause. The "men" in this means every man in your life. The "o" represents "on." The "pause" is like the pause button you push on your DVD player or VCR — you'll know what I mean. That means they will stop and shut the hell up!

Everything pauses when you go through menopause. Sex will pause — yes, it will stop at a screeching halt. Everything is put on hold, because you're going through all of these changes. You're hot one minute, you're cold the next. You're crying one minute, you're happy the next. Menopause can also be called schizophrenia. Never go to a psychologist when you're going through menopause. They'll put you on antipsychotic drugs when you're just going through a very natural progression in your life.

I've followed my momma's example. You know what, she embraced it. When she was going through it, she had herself a good time. She'd have her hot flashes, what she called her "personal summers" and all this other stuff. But she was pretty happy about it. She got to this point where she just thought she deserved it. When you can embrace it and not look at it as a terrible part of your life and take it gracefully, I do believe it can be a beautiful experience. But if you fight it, it will sure as hell put you on "pause" and fight you back.

So just like my mother, I embraced it. It also helps sometimes if you go and get one of those hormone shots or something to make you feel normal. But I think if you open your arms to it and take it for what it is, and again, laugh at it, it can represent a whole new place in your life. You can finally rest and relax and enjoy yourself and not have to worry from month to month — if you know what I mean.

Here's another thing: by the time you get to that point, you should really take it for what it's supposed to be meant for, because by that time you're running out of patience.

God knew to give it to you at this time of your life. You ain't got no more patience for any more children that can drive you crazy. If you had any more at this time, you would find out why some animals eat their young.

GETTING OLDER = GETTING BETTER

Since we've talked about menopause, I guess I may as well go on and talk about getting old. Do you know if you put Vaseline on your wrinkles, you don't need no Botox or face-lifts?

I feel like every day you get on this earth is a precious gift. If you do the best you can with that day, you have done the right thing. If you fight it, that's another thing. Here's what you have to understand about this life: every day you're supposed to grow older. Go on to where you're supposed to be in this life. Stop worrying about getting old. Everybody gets old — it's a natural progression. So many folks don't want to age. They're looking for the fountain of youth.

I remember this lady — she was my hair-dresser. She always used to say, "I don't want to see forty, I don't want to be forty!" Do you know what happened to that lady? She put that out into the universe, and it came back to her. Before she turned forty, she died of a brain aneurysm.

You have to embrace who you are. I want every year, every birthday God wants me to have. And every year through the last, I want to be better. You don't get older — you get better — if you're wise. Ain't nothing like an old fool, though. I can't stand to see somebody who is fifty still as stupid as they were when they were fifteen. Every year, you're supposed to learn something on this earth.

We go through these circles — I call it my "spin theory" . . . like when you're young, you're leaning and dependent on your parents to take care of you — then you get a little older and you spin to a different level. You're supposed to take care of yourself (I know all of us know somebody whose parents are still taking care of them and they're fifty-five). Then you get older and you have to lean and be dependent again. You get the opportunity to give back — every problem your kids gave to you, you get the opportunity to be that problem for them. It's a wonderful time. That's what they mean when they say, "Payback is a mother!"

I think getting older is also time that God himself has designed for us to go through these fragile stages where we know we're getting older — we know that we soon have to leave this earth — and it's time for us to walk closer with him and lean and depend on him

158

in the winters of our life.

You have to understand that getting old is a celebration. So many people don't make it. You look at all these young people dying today. Everything that happens to you in this life, if you conquer it, if you beat it, you've won. Embrace every day you get.

Let's talk about sex and old age. See, I thank God for old age because my bones and joints ache, and I can't bend over in those positions that I used to when I was younger. Thank God, because it is so embarrassing. Come to think of it, it was embarrassing then! I was just too young to know it. That's the good thing about getting old. Men can't ask you to do some of the things you used to do before. I can now say, "Baby, thank you for asking me to do that, but nowadays that chandelier ain't going to support me."

I tell you, one time, you remember that game Twister? Me and one of my husbands — I can't remember which one — the third or fourth — we would play Twister while we were having sex. One time, I had twisted so much I just . . . because, you know, I'm big and I'm tall . . . they had to call the ambulance to come and untwist me. That was pretty embarrassing. Had I used Vaseline before we started, there would have been no need for the Jaws of Life.

Getting older can open up a lot of doors for you. You get good seats at theaters. You tell them, "You know, I can't see too well — I got to get down close." And before you know it, you're down on the first row, even if the show's sold out. Dead smack in the middle — it's a wonderful thing. Because I got glaucoma medicine, I see pretty good, but I tell a lie because I want to be close. You know, you also get better parking spaces. You get to pull up at the front door (even though I've been doing that for years) in that hand-icapped spot. You get all kinds of benefits. And did you know that at Denny's you get a special on your breakfast the older you get. But come to think of it, if you keep eating at Denny's you might not get too much older. I'm just kidding — I love Denny's. So get old and enjoy yourself and eat good! Go to Denny's and have you a meal.

To find out if you're old or not, here's a test, part A and part B: Go to your bed and lay down. Ask yourself, Do I feel any pressure on my bones? Do I feel comfortable? Am I breathing normal? If all those answers are yes and you feel good, you've passed part A of the test. Now for part B, stand up out of the bed. Some of you need to get up slower than the others. Stand up. If you feel pressure on your bones and you feel like you can't make it to the bathroom, you might be old. That's how you can tell if you're old or not.

The minute I stand up and that weight hits them joints — and the knee bone connects to the anklebone — all the pressure of the world hits me. I realize I'm older just because everything just goes down, lower and lower and lower. I passed by a mirror one day coming out of the shower and said, "Good Lord, when did all of that happen? When is it going to stop getting lower?" That's when you know you're old, because when you were young, your butt was closer to your back. Now it's just below your knees.

DEATH: SOMETHING WE ALL GOT TO DO

People say when you're dead, you're done. I'm not so sure about that. I believe that you answer for everything that you've done on this earth. That's why I try to do right by people. I don't beat the hell out of them unless they mess with me. But for the most part, I'm nice.

Death is something that a lot of people have been afraid of, but it's something that we all got to do. Do me a favor. If you're getting close to death, please, please, get yourself some insurance, make sure your will is clear. Even if you're not close to death, you may think you're going to live to a hundred years, take care of these things. I'll tell you why. There ain't nothing like having a bunch of folks arguing over your stuff after you're dead. The least you can do is have some peace.

I had a cousin. She ain't bought no insurance. She ain't got no will. She ain't saved no money. She spent just enough and saved just enough to keep the bills going. She left all her stuff for somebody to be fussing and fighting over. At her funeral, they were arguing for forty-five minutes over her ring! They were trying to take it off the woman when she was laying there.

So I've learned to save a little money — put everything into perspective, so that when that time comes, your kin aren't arguing over who gets what. In my case, all they're going to get is my deep fryer, my glaucoma medicine, and, of course, a jar of Vaseline.

The best part about death is the life you've lived before. So every day that you're here, live, just live. I can't say this enough. You wonder why I keep repeating it? Because you really have to learn to enjoy your life! If I had made ten million dollars or five thousand dollars and it's all in the bank — and I'm dead, what the hell good was it for me?

So here's what I'm going to do: I'm going to save just enough to make sure that if I'm still around, I've got enough money — but I'm going to spend, too. I'm going to take trips, go to the casino, and have a good time. I have a wonderful friend who had brain surgery and cancer. They told her she had three months to live. She is doing fine, living well. Every time I talk to her, she's in another part of the world. When you come that close to death, you realize that if you get a second chance, you're going to do everything that you want to do. And she is doing it! She calls me every now and then to borrow some money, and I send it to her because I'm happy for her. But I tell her, "They told you three months and you been here for twelve years. You can't keep calling me and borrowing all this money — but I'm happy you're around."

So all of this is to say again, every day you get, make the best of it. When I leave, I don't want to leave owing nobody nothing. In fact, I'm having a closed coffin with a padlock on it. I don't want them looking at me or touching me. Yes, I want them to put a padlock on it with a combination that only I know. When it's time to get out, I'll give the combination to Jesus.

■ ■ ■ ■

PART SEVEN
MISS MADEA'S RULES OF
ETIQUETTE

■ ■ ■ ■

I wrote this chapter because I was watching Martha Stewart on television. She was doing all this beautiful decorating and giving all this very posh advice about how to behave, and I thought, Who the hell is she talking to? So I wanted to talk to some folks who don't know nothing about no twenty trillion billion dollars, folks who live on a shoestring budget. And what I mean by shoestring budget is, that's all you can afford — a shoestring.

ON MANNERS

I know I don't have to tell you this, but people don't have manners no more. Maria Shivery is dead. They don't say "thank you" and "please." I used to be nice but my niceness went out in the late '70s, when people started to change and be mean, stepping on you and full of road rage. Road rage comes from rap music, did you know that? If you don't want to have no road rage, don't put on rap, because it makes you speed up and run into something. You get real angry.

If I'm coming through a door, and they don't hold it for me, I say, "Thank you for holding the door." I make sure to give them what the psychologists call "a teachable moment."

I hate to get on the elevator and someone says, "Press seven," like I'm the elevator person. If you say, "Will you please press seven," or "Give me seven," I say, "Hell, I ain't working on this elevator, I'm just trying to go to my room, too." If they say, "Would you mind pressing seven?" and their hands are full, then I do it. I sure don't sit around pressing buttons like I'm announcing, "Lingerie department, floor seven." I ain't working at Sears.

ON TELLING SOMEONE TO IMPROVE THEIR HYGIENE

I don't know why we get so embarrassed telling people they don't smell too good. Now, there's a way to do it, and there's a way not to do it. First, don't do it in front of nobody, unless you don't like the person and are trying to embarrass them. If you see somebody with something in their nose or they ain't smelling good, don't let the person go out . . . unless, like I said, you don't like them. Now, I've let people go out there with their panty hose up in their underwear coming out of the bathroom because I didn't care. I didn't like them. But what you've got to do is be mindful. If it's somebody you like . . . even if it's somebody you don't know so well, pull them to the side and say, "Baby, go and clean your nose, go to the bathroom," or just say, "Go to the bathroom and check yourself out."

If somebody's got bad breath and you're

talking to them, they should get the hint when you keep turning your head away from them. If you're riding in the car with them and you've got your head out of the window like a collie, they ought to know something's wrong.

But if they don't, here's what you do: make sure you have some gum or some mints with you and you say, "Here, take a mint." If they say no, you say "Take the damned mint!" You make sure you offer it three or four times. "You're sure you don't want this mint? If I were you, and I was in your mouth, I would want this mint." If they don't take the hint, then they're crazy as hell, and they want to smell like that.

If you know somebody whose hygiene ain't that great, there are a couple of ways to tell them they need a bath. You can pull them to the side and say, "There's a couple of things you're doing I want to talk to you about." You can say things like, "What kind of soap you use? Why don't you try a new soap and see what happens. This soap has a different kind of fragrance. Here, I bought it for you. Here, you go test it out and tell me what you think." If they say something like, "I don't like this soap, I'm allergic to it, I can't use this kind of soap," then, well, hell, there ain't nothing you can do but get the hell away from them because you tried to tell them.

But what I like best is unspoken language. I like to speak without talking. The best thing you can do is take you some soap and send it to them in the mail with an anonymous note:

This is from all the people who want to remain your friend.
Use this soap before you see us again.
A poem for you.

With some people you've got to be blatantly honest. "Baby, you don't smell too good. Go over there and wash and scrub and get you some bleach." Back in the day, we used to take us a capful of bleach and put it in the bath in the water, just to make sure we got real clean. That's when you knew you were "squeaky clean." Children don't get squeaky clean no more, where you could rub behind the ears and actually hear it squeaking.

ON HOME DÉCOR

I have some tips on houses. I don't like a nasty house. Your house represents who you are. People ought to be able to walk into your house at any time and you not be embarrassed. You shouldn't have to run and clean up something — especially the public rooms, like your bathroom, your living room, the kitchen. These rooms need to be clean at all times. Now, your bedroom and closets can get a little junky. But there's a difference between being junky and nasty.

I had an aunt who was just nasty. You had to step over stuff that's been there for weeks and months . . . and flies. I don't understand that. You see, she had five maids, so I don't know why she was nasty. No, she didn't have five maids — she had five kids. I just call them maids because when they're that young, that's what they are. All you got to do is brainwash them early on and that will make them go and clean up.

I don't believe in no designer coming in your house telling you where to put the furniture. What the hell! Put the furniture where you want it to be. It's your house, you got to live in it, and you got to be happy when you walk in it.

In my house, you can put your feet up on anything, because everything's wrapped in plastic. Even the lampshade's still got the plastic on it — the sofa, the coffee table, everything. So in my house you can get comfortable. When you lay on the mattress in my bedroom, be careful you don't slide off because the sheet is on top of the plastic that the mattress originally came in.

Yes, everything in my house is fresh. Remember what I said about the Jheri curls. I learned that in the early '80s and never took the plastic off. You can just wipe it down.

ON HAVING HOUSEHOLD HELP

Those of us without maids — I mean children — can use some help from time to time.

You know what I've found about household help — you know, my mother used to do it — is that people have a life outside of you, and you have to remember that it's their job. All they're coming there for is to do their job — leave them the hell alone, tell them what you need done, and let them do their job.

A lot of times what the problem is, especially if you're in a position to have help, you feel like you're reaching out to the lesser and you're doing something to help a lesser person or you're trying to be a shining star. Let me tell you, those folks have a life. Because when they leave your house, you had better believe they ain't thinking about you. Treat them with respect because people are people. Just because you got a little more than somebody else, don't mean that you are better. And you know, life is strange. You could be surprised. You could end up working for that person — so you need to be careful how you treat folks.

Some people are so crazy that they clean up the house before the maid comes. That's like pre-washing dishes before you put them in the dishwasher. I ain't doing that, either. If the dishwasher can't take all the food off, oh well, you'll be eating leftovers with your next meal.

ON ENTERTAINING GUESTS

The main thing I want my house to be when you come into it is comfortable. *But not so comfortable that you want to stay.* The trick is to make these people comfortable enough to stay for a little while. You don't want your house to be so comfortable that people walk in and just automatically want to stay and even worse — fall asleep. That's a problem. So what you do is you make the sofa really, really nice and really comfortable and put some really nice pillows on it so when people come into your living room and sit, they're really comfortable.

Get out your highlighters, you will want to underline this. In fact, you may want to send me a thank-you note after you read this. If the worse case happens and your guests want to stay overnight, here's how you keep their visit short and sweet. The guest bed needs to be the cheapest, hardest mattress you can find in your life. As a matter of fact, put a couple of pieces of plywood in between your sheets and your bed and put a little piece of foam on top of it.

What I have to tell you now is worth the cost of this book alone. This works when all else fails. Take a piece of dead fish, preferably a fish head. Get you one of those nice fragrance-scented candles and carefully stuff the dead fish inside it, so when you light the candle, the heat will give your guest just the right mix between the delicate smell of flowers and the rotten fish.

If you want the person to stay for just a couple of days, make sure you don't let them see the fish head. They shouldn't know it's there. You want them to go in the room and start sniffing around, trying to figure out what the smell is but never find it. The best thing to do is you take your nice carving utensils from the kitchen that you use to grate carrots or apples. You cut out the bottom of the candle, and shave out enough wax to get the head of the fish inside. So, in the beginning, the candle smells good, but pretty soon, sure enough, the odor begins to come out.

This way, the people will come and visit

but never stay. You never want anybody to come and stay too long. Any good, smelly fish will do, but from my long experience, the head of a catfish is ugly with those whiskers, so that's the best head to use. You can always find them in the 'hood because everybody's always got catfish somewhere. Put the catfish inside the vanilla-scented candle and light it. That's your Madea Stewart tip for living . . . alone.

If this is not enough, then take the draperies and you spray them down with a little cat piss, just a little — just a hint of cat piss at the bottom of the draperies. When the breeze comes through from the window, they will smell nothing but feline pee-pee and want to le-leave.

ON BEING A GOOD HOST

If you have guests coming over and you want to impress them, what I suggest you should do is go to your kitchen and get out a bowl of Cap'n Crunch. You take the Cap'n Crunch and sprinkle it with powdered sugar. You take some mayonnaise and put it on some bread and cut it into four quarters. You trim the crusts on one half. On the other half, you leave it. It's recommended to use Wonder bread. . . . I don't know if they still make Wonder bread . . . take your bread and leave it out in the open for a little while, and it will get really, really hard. I'm sorry, but people who have dentures or anything like that, they won't be able to handle it. You put all the bread and mayonnaise along the edge of your nicest plate. Put the Cap'n Crunch and cinnamon in the middle and you bring it out and set it on the table. These are called watercress croissants. Share with your guests how you meticulously prepared this special recipe early that morning. They will appreciate it and will be impressed that it was not bought at 7-Eleven.

Again, whatever you pour to drink for them, make sure that it does not taste so good that they'll want to come back. Let me clarify this. It should taste decent, but it shouldn't taste great. Remember, the point here is that you don't want people to come back. The main thing with guests is that you want them to stay "a little while." You want them to come, be comfortable for a minute, but get the hell out. Please, remember, you don't want them to stay.

Now that people know my secrets of how to get rid of a guest, they might be trying to do that to me. I'm a person who feels uncomfortable in a lot of people's houses, going over and relaxing, taking off my shoes and all that other stuff. Sometimes, I'll take a fish head over to their house and leave it in the corner, so they'll think, "Oh, something's wrong." I say, "I can't stay here," and get my suitcases out the door quick. I don't like being at other people's houses.

ON ACCIDENTAL NUDITY

It may be a big deal for you if somebody accidentally sees your Frisbee, but not me. It ain't embarrassing for me if someone walks in on me in the bathroom. It's more embarrassing for the person who walked in to see all of this.

I scarred my seven-year-old nephew. One time, he ran out of there and just peed all over himself. I guess he had never seen that many folds and wrinkles and lines on anybody. He's autistic now.

Those kind of situations can be tough, but you have to make the person comfortable afterward. So, what I do, what I did to him afterward, I come in and make a joke before they get a chance to say anything. It makes them relax and laugh a little bit, because otherwise they'll be embarrassed and hurt and crying . . . or suicidal.

It may be traumatic for the other person, but I'm used to it. Remember, I used to be a stripper. See, when I look at me sometimes . . . you see, I had this dream. I'll be just running, running like Forrest Gump, and everything is tight and firm and nothing's really bouncing. It's all just tight. Then I'll wake up. And I'll be, like, damned, who was that? That's the person I want to be, but them days is over. I look in the mirror and say, "She's under there somewhere." Every day, it feels like something has snuck up on you, you know what I'm saying. "Where did that happen? I ain't never seen that."

ON PARTIES

I don't have parties at my house anymore, and I'll tell you why. People will come up and tear up all your stuff. Every bit of it will just be tow up. I used to have parties and have folks over but then they'd come in and be dropping cigarettes. By the time the party was halfway getting started, I'd be beating folks up and fighting because they'd be dropping cigarettes on my sofa, pouring drinks all over everything. Even plastic covers can't stop the damage from people who don't know how to behave.

You know you're at a really good party, you know, in Beverly Hills and Hollywood, when they give you a gift when you come in and out. I was looking at Oprah's fiftieth birthday party — she had it at the Hotel Bel-Air and then she went to Santa Barbara and had it in a tent. They spent all this money on this party. You ain't have to do all of that to still have a good time.

Here's the formula. Try it the next time you're having a party. All you have to do is call two people that you know and say B.Y.O.B — bring your own bottle. What happens is you tell two people, and they tell two more people, and they call two more people, and before you know it, all these folks will show up at your house. That way, you have saved a ton of money on liquor.

All those Cap'n Crunch sandwiches you have left over that your earlier guests didn't eat will come in handy. Put them out on the table, and you've saved even more money.

You can even turn any festive occasion into a moneymaking opportunity. What we used to have was rent parties to pay our rent. You'd charge everybody. They'd bring their own bottle, and you charge them two or three dollars to come in. All you need is a deck of cards and you can make another $1,200 playing tonk — T-O-N-K. And you sit there and you get four people to play and then put their money up. Every game, they have to pay the house two or three dollars. So you make a ton of money for having a good party.

ON THE ART OF COOKING

They talk about the "art of cooking." They put it on TV like it's glamorous. Hell, I've been cooking for fifty-five years. I'm tired of damned cooking. If I can't fry it and get it quick, I don't want to eat it. You look around and see these people cooking on TV, talking about "you add dez seasoning" and "isn't dis vonderful." What the hell, that's somebody who ain't been cooking all his life.

When I was too young to cook, my mother would do it. She would make these collard greens, mash potatoes, ham hocks. Thanksgiving she'd cook 7UP cake, tea cakes — huu, them was the good days when I didn't have to cook. Ham, fried turkey — we used to drop it down in the deep fry.

It's a different story when you get older and you have to cook for your sisters and brothers and then for your daddy when he comes in and for your momma, then cook for your child — and my daughter was a big girl — I had to cook a lot for her. I would wake up cooking and go to bed cooking. I was so glad when she learned how to order a pizza. It was so hard for me to keep on cooking and working as hard as I was.

For all of us who don't have time to cook, that's why I'm writing a cookbook, so you can master the art of cooking food that will be filling, but not good tasting so people will want to stay or ask for second helpings. Along with Cap'n Crunch and perhaps my secret recipe for sweet potato pie, you will find other things to do with leftovers and leave-behinds.

ON GETTING BAD SERVICE

I ain't one for diplomacy. If I go to a restaurant or the cleaners and get bad service, that person is going to have a bad day. I've been ignored a whole lot of times going in places to buy cars, going to the grocery store, cleaners, and everything. I'll say something. I'm not the kind of person that will sit around because it will make me mad, and I'll carry it with me. I'm going to get it off my chest right there.

If you ain't treating me right, I'm going to tell you personally. "Look, you need to be doing a better job." If you still have an attitude, then I'm going to find your boss and we all are going to have a talk. And if that don't work, I'm going to set it off in there. They're going to know I'm mad. I'm going to cause such a scene that the corporate office is going to find out who the hell was there and what happened. But the first thing you try to do is talk to the person.

I can't stand going up to the window of

those fast food restaurants. I had this one little girl just staring at me. I'm waiting for her to say, "May I help you?" She was just standing there looking. So I just stood there for seven minutes just looking at her like she was crazy as hell. Then she says, "What you want?" Then I say, "That's not how you start with an order. You say, 'May I help you?'" Then she hemmed and hawed. "May I help you?" Okay. I ordered the food and everything. Then she put it into a bag and kind of threw it to me. I snatched her from behind that counter and beat the hell out of her.

Now every time I walk in there, you know what she says? "Hello, may I help you? Welcome." Sometimes, you have to teach people the rough way. I don't mind setting it off so folk will learn you can't treat everybody crazy. I do it for two occasions — being a woman and being black. People will mess around and think they can talk to you any kind of way they want to. You got two strikes against you. That gets me fighting more than anything else. You ain't going to treat me that way because you think I'm less than. That ain't going to happen.

What a lot of folk will do is just walk out and don't come back to the place no more. They'll drive across town to another place. I'm not going to do that. You've got to get it fixed in your neighborhood because it's usually the worst there. I can go to certain neighborhoods where the money is at and everybody's just nice and smiling and happy when you walk up in the restaurant. Then I go in the 'hood and they're acting like I'm crazy, like, "What you want!" So I want it fixed in my neighborhood and I'm going to say something — I don't care if they don't like it.

■ ■ ■ ■

PART EIGHT
MADEA'S REAL-LIFE
SURVIVAL TIPS

■ ■ ■ ■

For those who believe that black women do what they like but not what they need to do . . .

MO' MONEY, MO' PROBLEMS

You want to talk about money? I ain't got none. But I can dream. So let's talk about money. This is what I learned about money. People say, "If I could be rich, if I could be rich, if I could be rich . . ." I don't know if I would want that. All I want is to have enough to do what I want to do, because mo' money, mo' problems.

That's why I like checks. Let's talk about checks. I keeps me some checks around so I can write them. But I miss back in the day when you would write the check and you had five days to get the money in the bank. Because checks are for people who ain't got no money. You were trying to wait to get the money but you still need the lights on.

Here's one of my favorite old tricks. Sometimes, I would write a check, and, dear me, I would be so absentminded that I would forget to sign it. Of course, I wouldn't forget,

I'd just act like I forgot to sign it — then go out and make the money and put it into the bank, to keep the lights on and food in the refrigerator. It's one good way you don't have no bounced checks going around.

But now this electronic stuff has messed up everything. Checks go through in fifteen minutes — and that works on my nerves. Hell, I can't even get me a good hustle going on no more. As long as I've got enough money to be all right, I'm good with that. All those husbands with all the insurance made me feel pretty good.

Here's another Madea secret that you shouldn't ever use, because crime does not pay. It's simple — the checks I was writing wasn't but fifteen dollars or twenty-five dollars. You know, you stay below a certain amount of money, you don't get time — it's just a misdemeanor. So if you go around and write a thousand checks for fifteen dollars, you'll be all right.

I'm sure you will believe me when I tell you they won't let me have no credit charges. That Sears card was the end of it. Take it from me, your children got to watch their credit. They got to make sure they do the right thing, because my credit is jacked up. I think, you know, they give you a score. And I think mine is 2. Try to buy a car with that!

So I tell the children, "Don't go out there messing up your credit." Take your time. Do the right thing. That credit's going to score you and everything in life — it ain't black, it ain't white, it's the credit.

Let me tell you the truth. God has provided for me, everything I ever needed, every day. See, a little becomes a whole lot if you have some good common sense. A lot of folks — I sit around and look at people, you know, wanting all the fancy stuff . . . I looked at this woman, used to live down the street from me. I ain't even know the woman. I met her long before I knew that she lived down the street. She had a beautiful car, diamond earrings — oooh, she had designer clothes on, and all this kind of stuff. Every time you'd see her she'd look good, hair was done, nails done — just a beautiful, beautiful black woman. One day, I was driving and I saw her getting out of her car, going into her house. She was acting like she didn't see me. So I got out and went up and started talking to her. She goes up to the door. It's her apartment. She's living in the projects! And I'm sitting there wondering how the hell you get all this stuff living in the projects!

If you're going to make money, do the right thing with it. Get you some hard assets.

Get you a house. That's what I did when I was bringing home so much cash from stripping — I bought me a house and I bought me a car so I could have something. Some equity before I started buying all those foolish things — but you ain't going catch me in that Calvin Klein and Ver-casey and all that stuff. Hell . . . I can't afford that, and I'm not going to act like I can.

Even if I could go into those stores, it's very expensive. Because of my size, what I have to do is I've got to buy *two.* I sew one on the front and one on the back. See, that's why I can't afford it. Hell, it's double for me. I walked up and saw a friend of mine — she had a seven-hundred-dollar dress — I said, "A seven-hundred-dollar dress for a damned rag." I look at J.Lo, she had that thing on, that Versace worth all those thousands of dollars on. Hell, please!

Me? I have a little extra money, I treat my-self to something fried. And a little glaucoma medicine, got to make sure my eyes are right, so I can see to enjoy my life. That's it. Then I put the rest of it aside, because every day the sun don't shine. You got to have something for when it rains.

I'm what you call "tight." You can't borrow no money from me. My cousin Irene . . . was it Irene that borrowed that twenty dollars from me? Yeah. She died, and I went to her funeral and tore up the whole casket because I was mad at her for dying, for not giving me my money back. People thought I was crying and upset. I wanted my twenty dollars back and I thought they had put it in her pocket, because her daughter buried her with some earrings on. So I took those earrings off and pawned them and got my twenty dollars back. I'm tight. I hold on to my money. I have to have something for when the slow times come.

It's crazy. What the hell, I don't understand why you want somebody's name on your butt, on your breast, on your hips, in your hair, on your feet — just crazy! I don't understand why people want to spend all this money on something . . . because they're paying little kids twenty cents to make those things over in some country . . . and you're a fool enough to buy them for nine hundred and eight hundred dollars. But what the hell — if you got real money, where you can afford all that stuff — so that fifty dollars to me is like five hundred to you, then be my guest and go out and buy that stuff.

But if you're living in the projects, pulling up in your car and you ain't got no garage — and you can pay eighty thousand dollars for

191

it and it's got wheels that spin on it, some-thing is wrong, and you got to figure out what your priorities are. If you got it, be that. You ain't got to act like it, because every-body knows you got it. If you ain't got it, go somewhere and sit down. Stop acting like you got it when you don't.

Remember I got to buy two to sew them together to make sure they fit right? That's always been the thing. See, I do all my shop-ping at the Wal-Mart. I can always find what I need at a good price. I'm the new spokesperson for Wal-Mart! So if you want bargains, that's where you go.

All these people who come over from these other countries, and they open up a shop in the neighborhood. Then they take all the money out of the neighborhood and go where they want to live. I can't sit there and blame anybody else, because it's black peo-ple more than anything else. If we open our own stores and did our own stuff in the neighborhoods and treated people with some respect and treated them right, people would come back. I can't necessarily blame nobody else for coming in and taking out and mistreating. You're only going to let folk do what they do to you. There come a time and a place when you'll have a say and you can change things.

BEING A SUCCESSFUL STRIPPER AND OTHER BUSINESS OPPORTUNITIES

What I am about to tell you about is just in case you want to walk a little bit on the wild side, like I did, and become a professional exotic dancer.

There's no big secret here, just a simple fact. Black men like big women — the thicker, the better. So the more cellulite, the more you can shake. When I touch my ankle and it jiggles all the way up my body, the more money I can make. It's about the jiggle. Jiggling is where it is. You've heard that song "You're Jiggling, Baby"? That was because he saw me. He saw me jiggling and went and wrote that song. It's like Jell-O. Jell-O is the root of jiggle. You got to understand that. Now you got some Ebonics history!

Back in the day, when I was a stripper, I got a lot of offers to do what they called them "stag films." They wanted me to do a few films. *Madea Does Mobile. An Officer and Madea. Madea and Harry Potter-er.* All of them, they wanted me to do, but I turned them down. I didn't want nothing permanent on film. It's one thing to go into the clubs and strip for a few folks . . . but then to have thousands of people buying it? I still get offers. They still call me because, you know, folks are into old nasty stuff. Some people want a big, old nasty woman. I've heard about some of that stuff on the Internet. It's just crazy as hell. I don't understand it. Backstairs-grandma.com. They wanted me to open that Web site. I said hell no.

RUN-INS WITH THE PO-PO

That's another good thing about getting old. If you run into the right policeman and you cry good enough and you act old enough, you might get away with it. But they know me in my town. They look at me and say, "Uhm, uhm, you know you been doing wrong." But sometimes, they say, "She's old and crazy, so we'll let her go." So it's a good thing. You know, you can get away from a few tickets by crying.

I saw this old lady on *The World's Scariest Police Chases.* This is true. She was in a car. The police pulled her over, and she was so nervous, she got out of the car and left the motor running! When she got out, the car took off and knocked her over. The police were running down the street trying to catch the car. She didn't get a ticket. It worked! So I tried that one time — acted like I was so upset that he pulled me over that I kept it in drive and it just ran off. And, sure enough, he didn't give me a ticket.

I don't mess with the po-po. I always play crazy with them, because that's what you got to do to get them to leave you alone. All of them act like they have an attitude, like they just woke up on the wrong side of the bed. They're always mad.

Hell yes, there's such a thing as racial profiling. Every time I leave the house, they look at me and say, "Hmm, that's a black woman." They all don't just see a woman in a Cadillac riding on twenties with the stereo system booming. They don't see that. They see a black woman . . . me.

SLIPPING AND FALLING AND OTHER ACTS OF PUBLIC LARCENY

I can't say I'm proud of everything I've done. I did some foolish things. For example, I've done a whole bunch of things to get free meals at restaurants. I've put salt in wine. I've brought bugs in with me. But that was back in the day — I don't do that stuff no more. *Huuu!* Don't talk about a buffet! I'd have my purse full of stuff and walk out of there and tell them I didn't like this or that — cause a whole scene and have the manager come.

You know what else I'm good at — slipping and falling. I've sued a lot of places — God, I used to love to slip and fall. I used to send my daughter when she was about nine years old — I'd tell her, I'd say, "Cora, just go in there and spill something on the floor, and I'm coming in a few minutes behind you. I went in there and walked up every aisle looking for her, looking by the pickle juice and all the stuff that can leak, you know, sodas and everything. I find her over on the cookie aisle. She had eaten thirteen thousand dollars' worth of cookies. So I had to slip to pay the bill. I got my lawsuit, got my settlement — $14,785. You see, they had taken me with the ambulance to the hospital. I didn't know she was still in there eating cookies. They didn't find her until two days later. So they had taken the cookies out of my settlement. That's when I stopped doing this.

TROUBLE-FREE ON PUBLIC TRANSPORT

If you have to go through a rough neighborhood on a bus or a train, there's something you need to remember. It's really simple. Look crazy as hell. If you're coming from work and you don't want to be bothered by nobody, I do my own version of what you see a lot of corporate women do when they take their work shoes off and put tennis shoes on. Here's what I change into: put your nastiest wig on your head and wrap yourself in some dirty old, run-down coat, put some dirty shoes on, and put them on whatever you're wearing, and sit there on that bus and mumble to yourself — ain't nobody going to bother you. That's the key to get to where you're going. Just to be extra safe, don't take it off until you get home.

The other thing — keep your eyes wide open. Don't be sleeping. They'll rob everything you've got if they think you're sleeping. You might wake up dead.

PUBLIC RESTROOM DOS AND DON'TS

I don't know why the Centers for Disease Control aren't talking about this. Toilet seats in public restrooms can be a great health menace unless you practice prevention and precaution. Here's what I have learned: if you have to go into a public restroom and they don't have any of those seat protectors to cover the seat, there's something that you can use . . . Vaseline on the toilet seat. You might slip and slide around and miss your mark, but I'm telling you, it's safe — it will kill any bacteria. You just rub it on the top and wipe it off. It cleans up everything, especially in the public restrooms.

If you forgot your Vaseline, women, this is what I suggest you do. Do not sit down on the toilet. Stand up! How you do this? you wonder. You have to have strong knees and strong feet and anklebones and your hamstrings and quads must be really strong. Some women already know what I'm talking about. You don't touch the toilet; you just get six or seven inches above it. Just aim and shoot.

You know what's funny, I've been in those positions where you've got both hands holding up your pants trying to keep them out of the cesspool on the floor. You're trying to keep your balance and do what you have to do — and here comes some idiot knocking on the door talking about, "Is anyone in there?" What the hell you think I'm doing in here, riding the pony? I'm trying to use the bathroom. That's why you should always keep you some Vaseline, so you never have to do what I call "ride the pony."

That's why it takes women forty-five minutes to use the bathroom, because they are riding the pony. They can't just go in there and stand up in there like the men do — shake and wash their hands and leave. No, they have to go in, wait for other women to ride the pony, and then finally get their turn to ride the pony. So as you're riding the pony, remember that you're doing two very important things: you're working your thigh muscles for exercise and you're saving your life by not touching the toilet seat.

STAYING CLEAN IF YOU ARE
A LARGE WOMAN

I told you early on that we were going to deal with some uncomfortable things in this book. This may be in the category of too much information for those of you who are skinny, but a public service for the rest of you — and you know who you are. The secret to getting clean when you're overweight is, number one, you can't shower. *Never* take a shower and think you're clean. You have to soak. You have to sit in a tub. You put a capful of Vaseline in the tub, especially if you're big, take the Vaseline and rub it all over the sides so you can move around. Okay?

Now listen, advisory number two, be careful. If you're over-over-overweight, don't put too much water in the tub, because it's going to be all over the floor, and not on your body. To repeat, you need to use the Vaseline to lube up the tub, sit down in the water, and soak. If the water cools off, put in some more hot water. You have to soak because there's no way to reach all those crevices and cracks that you can't even reach with your hand.

If you're married, it's okay to ask, "Baby, can you wash the back of my knees, because I can't get to them?" If somebody loves you, they get in there and clean with you. And there are lots of men who are into cleaning and will get down on their knees to help you.

If there are areas that you are still not able to clean, and you just wash and wash and wash, and they're still filthy, here's your remedy: Get some sandpaper and rub a little Vaseline on it. Vaseline will smooth out and soften the sandpaper so it will work just fine. Wash gently in the area of the buildup. You might see a little discoloration, a little redness, but after it's all done, you'll stay clean for about thirty-eight days. That doesn't mean that you can get away with bathing once a month. Best to bathe three times a day.

Again, showers and big people are a no-no, unless the shower flows from every direction. Handheld showers won't work because you can only wash the front — you can't reach to wash the back. The bigger you are, the more you have to bathe.

BUYING THINGS FROM TV

You know, I used to look at those introversials, whatever you call them. I used to buy all that stuff. I had this one product — you rub it on you to lose weight, you rub it on and go to sleep and wake up thinner. I spent a whole bunch of money on that — it was nothing but Vaseline, what I found out. I was mad as hell.

They'll fool you. See, the older you get, they'll call you up with all kinds of crazy stuff. I don't buy that. I did buy that J.Lo ring that they had on QVC, the replica that Ben Affleck gave to J.Lo. I bought two or three of them.

I bought the Thighmaster — it didn't work for me. No, my thighs mastered getting bigger. It's hard as hell to be pushing your legs up and down. That's nasty. I don't like pushing all that stuff together like that. You know how women have that little air when they're young. You look at them when they're walking down the street — they've got that air in between their legs. I don't have that air. I've never had that air. My thighs rub together. So I thought that would help me. But I need a bulldozer or something to get these right. Master these thighs! It ain't going to be no Thighmaster. If this is a problem for you, again, refer back to the chapter on Vaseline.

HAVING PETS AS A SURROGATE FAMILY

I don't have any pets because they're almost as much trouble as a husband or a child. But I guess before I let a person come into my house and drive me crazy, I'll go get one. If you're sitting in your place and you're paying the bills and a person is making you crazy every day, you should get a dog, too. The dog ain't going to talk back. I say, "Sit down," and it's going to go over there and get out of the way.

Do you know they offer insurance for pets? Back in my day, if the dog dies, the dog is dead. If he needed surgery, he was going blind, you'd say, "Oh, well, the dog's going blind, he's blind, crippled, and crazy" — there's nothing you could do. Now, they're putting the dog into surgery. They have hotels for dogs, day care centers for dogs. I just look at all these people spending all this money on a dog and say, "Wow." It's crazy as hell. I just don't understand it.

Better yet, what about a hamster or a goldfish in the corner? Yes, if I ever get a pet, that's all it would be . . . a goldfish. Something I could wave at and look at every now and then, who ain't going to bark and tear up the rug and piss all over everywhere. A goldfish is just fine.

SEEING THE WORLD

I don't like to fly because it's too dangerous for me. I don't like being up in that air. I don't like nobody putting me inside a bullet, putting me on a runway, pulling the trigger, and just letting it land wherever it's supposed to. That's what it feels like to me. I prefer to stay on the ground. The easiest way to see the world is to just go to one place — Disney World. I go to Disney World and tour all the different cities they have. I've been everywhere, all over the world, through Disney World.

But there's another problem for me about airplanes, being a woman with a full figure. You could tell when you're walking down the aisle, if you're big, you can count every row because your hips are hitting on both sides. So when the lady says, "Go down to row eighteen," you don't even have to look up. You just count, "One, two, three . . ." as your hips hit. You figure out where you're going.

You can tell when you're getting close to your seat because there's a man sitting there, or a woman sitting there, who's saying (or better yet, praying), "Lord, I hope she ain't going to sit here. . . . I hope she ain't going to sit here." And I say, "Excuse me, that's my seat." You see them start blowing, huffing, and puffing. Of course, then, I sit down in the middle seat between two people. They always put me in the middle. Now, they know damned well they should have looked at me when I got to the counter, and said, "Ma'am, we need to put you in an exit row all by yourself or something." I hate a full flight.

Now, me, my human body fits in the chair.

But all that extra stuff, those pound cakes and shortcakes and fried everything was over here . . . half in his seat and in the other. He got mad and went storming up to the front saying, "She needs to get another . . . she needs to buy another seat," just going off. They asked me to get off the plane. They didn't know who they were talking to. I set it off over there. I said hell no, all these airlines around here trying to make all this money, making these seats too small for real people. "There ain't no big people in America? In America, there's an epidemic, and I ain't buying no two damned tickets. You're going to put me on this plane. And I'm going where I got to go. I ain't getting off."

So, they called all the FBI and talking about that I was a terrorist trying to blow the plane up. I didn't say I was going to blow it up. I said I was going to bust up the captain and everybody else in there if they didn't let me on that plane.

I don't like people talking about being fat as a disability. It ain't no damned disability. Hell, you did that. A disability is something that you ain't have no control over. You can control that fat. But I still ain't going to buy two plane tickets. I got one and you can all move me up to first class or something. You can buy me two tickets if you don't want me sitting next to you.

I've never broken any furniture by sitting down on it. But once I sat down in a rocking chair and got up, and the chair was still there. And I didn't even know it walking into the kitchen. That's pretty embarrassing. I remember when I used to go to my daughter's school for the PTA meetings. We used to have to sit in those itty-bitty chairs. That was painful as hell. I believe I still got one stuck somewhere up there but I ain't seen it.

THE BEAUTY SALON

Let me tell you something. In the black world, there's the church, the beauty shop, and the barbershop. If you know any information — if you want to save your soul, go to church. If you want to go to hell, go to the beauty shop or the barbershop.

That's where all the garbage, the lying, the cheating — you can find out who did what to who. No matter what's going on in the community, just sit there for a few minutes — you don't even have to say a word, just sit there with your head down, you'll find out about everybody in the town.

I just sit around and listen, because that's how you figure it out. Somebody will come in upset, and they'll be talking about themselves. Don't go up there and say nothing about yourself, thinking the people there are your friends. Believe me, it's going to be all over the beauty salon. Then it's all over the city. You see, a hairdresser and a bartender are like therapists, because black folk can't always afford all these things. So you sit there and you're telling everything that's going on. Before you know it, all your business is around. So I learned to sit there and keep my mouth shut and get my hair done. If you just open your ears, all the stuff you hear around you is crazy. It's more entertaining than TV. It's like Jerry Springer without all the foolishness — because I was going to a nice spot without all that fighting and all that carrying on.

There's an unwritten rule that as soon as you finish telling your stuff and you walk out the door, it's the green light to pass it along to everybody else. Then there's another little game that happens — you find that they want to act like they're your friend — "Girl, you know what they're saying about you, I wouldn't take that." You see, that's how they start. Then they start a whole bunch of mess. Next time you see the person that started it, you're ready to fight. "She's coming to get her hair done, let me check the appointment book. She'll be here Thursday at nine if you want to come see her." Because, you see, they like all that drama. The more drama going on in the place, the more money they make!

The quality of the information means your hair can look like hell, but you got all the dirt in the neighborhood by sitting up in there for two hours. That's right. You go to Suzy's Salon, because if you want to know anything, that's where it is. It's especially good to go in before Friday night, so you know what man in the neighborhood to mess with and who not to mess with, who's single that week and who ain't.

■ ■ ■ ■

PART NINE
MADEA'S COMMENTARY ON
THE GOOD BOOK

(NOT THIS ONE)

■ ■ ■ ■

Everybody needs a little Jesus . . . not too much, just enough.

My Favorite Bible Story

I love the Bible story when Peter was walking on the water. He was in the boat with the twelve disciplines. And Jesus said, "It is I and come to me," and Peter said, "If that be You, let me come out." And the Bible said that they were sore afraid, which meant they were so scared that it hurt. Peter got out of the boat and started walking toward Jesus on the water. He got distracted, and he started to sink. He took his eyes off Him.

So I wanted to know what would make Peter take his eyes off Jesus in a situation like that. So I searched the prescriptions for myself. I went to the book of Geronimo and found out that Jonah was in the belly of the whale. As Peter was walking on the water, the whale was swimming right by him. He looked down. I realized something at that moment: when you got your own situation, you can't worry about somebody else's deliverance.

So that was a great moment for me. I thought that Jesus would rescue Peter out of the water, but He didn't. He left him there. The Bible says He left him there for forty days and forty nights. He said, "I am going to send you a comforter." Guess who came there to get him? Noah on the ark! Noah pulled him up out of the water. God will always send a rescue boat for you.

You've got to pick up your Bible. If you haven't seen that story, you've got to read your Bible. It's a blessing.

THE LORD HELPS THOSE . . .

I don't like a whole bunch of folks sitting around talking about, "Oh, God's going to make a way, God's going to make a way," and they ain't doing nothing. The Bible says, "Faith without work is dead." That means you got to get up and do something. People a lot of times try to hide behind Jesus instead of getting out front and let Him push or lead you to where you need to be. You know, I have strong opinions about this. If religious people would just read the Bible, sometimes they'd get the answers to a lot of their questions.

SINNERS

Let's be perfectly clear. I think everybody on this earth messes up. I don't care who it is. It can be from a preacher to the Pope. They all sin from day to day to day.

Here's the secret. The main thing is keeping a balance — that you're not doing so much sin that you're no good to anybody — so you don't have any good in your life. And not going around trying to be so good and thinking you're perfect — then you're just as useless as the sinner. So it's about keeping a balance between the two of them.

GOING TO CHURCH, READING THE BIBLE, AND PRAYING

You know, I don't go to church no more. I used to go to church. Let me tell you something about church. You know, church is fine, but my problem is *church folk.* If you ever go to church looking for anything but God, you're in trouble, because church folk will run you out of there. I have never had so many people sitting around and talking and pointing their fingers and all that other stuff, acting like they're holier than everybody else. But if God ever uncovered their dirt, it would blow your mind! The things that they do! So you got to watch people who are pointing fingers all the time. When they're pointing one at you, the other fingers are pointing back at themselves. So I stopped going a long time ago.

213

I'm thinking about going back. I'm getting a little older — the older you get, the closer you need to get to God. If I keep eating all these fried foods, I'll be seeing Him sooner than I think. So I may need to go in there and get acquainted with the Big Fellow.

I read the Bible, but I don't know what it is — as soon as I open that Bible and I look down at Jesus's letters in red, I say, Jesus was talking too much — and I close it and go to bed, because He talks too much. Every page I would turn to everything is red, red, red, red, red. I'd say, "Jesus, can You please just be quiet for just a little while?" But he talked a whole bunch, didn't He? I used to read Segagenesis and Revelatia and Heroes and all them other books in the Bible — Chapter 4, the Palms, and the Book of Jobs, the New Testaments. You know, I read all of them.

I pray every day. I pray every time I get stopped by the police. I pray like you would not believe. Every red light, when they pull me over, I say, "Lord, please don't let them find that warrant." "Did I pay that last ticket, Jesus?" "Did they catch up with me for my last husband?" So, yes, I pray all the time. "Lord, please let this check go through." I pray all the time, yes, I do. Nine times out of ten, my prayers don't get answered, because somebody told me I was praying for the wrong things. But every now and then, I'll get lucky.

TURN THE OTHER CHEEK, AND THEN . . .

My mother was crazy as hell. I don't know if she was literally bipolar, but the older she got, the weirder she got. But she passed on a lot of good traits to me. She was a strong woman — she ain't take no stuff. She passed on that "beat the hell out of them first and ask questions later" — yeah, that's my motto. Beat first and ask questions later. I'm like the Inglewood Police Department.

Turn the other cheek. That's what the Bible says. That's what Jesus said. And if they hit you again, you turn the other one. He didn't tell you what to do when you've turned both of them. So I take it upon myself, at that point, to kick some ass. It depends on — if I'm in the wrong, I'll take a little lick. It ain't going to be from no man. I ain't talking about no physical hitting, I'm talking about something that someone's doing to you. I'll take it if I'm in the wrong. There'll be no physical hitting. That makes me crazy, makes me go to jail.

So follow closely now, because this is important. The New Testament says, "Turn the other cheek." The Old Testament says, "An eye for an eye." This really ain't confusing.

They're really saying the same thing.

Jesus says, "Turn the other cheek," and then "turn the other cheek." After you've run out of cheeks, you will find a little arrow by the text saying, "Refer to the Old Testament." The Holy Spirit itself will whisper to you, "Refer to the Old Testament, from Genesis to Malakai." That will tell you what to do next.

■ ■ ■ ■

PART TEN
MADEA SPEAKS HER MIND

■ ■ ■ ■

Speak your mind or lose it!

PEACE IN THE HOUSE

There are two places you are supposed to have peace — one is in your house and the other is in the grave. And since I'm not in a rush to get to the second one, it may as well be my house. If you ain't ready to go to the grave, you need to go into your house and get rid of everything that's in there that ain't giving you peace . . . or send it to its grave. Just keep the goldfish.

It has been said that your house is your castle. Some people have little bitty castles and some have big castles. Whatever your castle is, no matter how big or small, it should be a place of peace. When you walk in and close that door from the outside world, everything that comes into your house you should be able to control, be it from the television or through a window. Control it or it will control you.

I don't understand how you can work all

day, pay all your bills, do all that you have to do to walk in the door, and have a whole bunch of hell break loose. That is crazy as hell. Your house is supposed to be a place where you can rest and relax and have peace of mind, with nobody in there driving you crazy. If they're in there, they need to get the hell out.

At your job, in traffic, walking on the street, riding the bus — they work on your nerves. This world is full of people who are here for the specific purpose to try to drive you crazy. Just turning on CNN and seeing the president, that works on your nerves. So you have to have a place in this world that you can call your sanctuary.

So I'm going to give you some tips on how to make your house a peaceful home. Get rid of your children, husband, family members, and friends and live by your damned self! That way, when you walk in, you'll be at peace. Nobody's bothering you. Might be lonely after a while — oh, well. If you don't want to be that extreme, then the people who are in your house will have to be subjected to some rules.

(Let me preface this by saying these rules are for the people who pay the bills! He or she who makes the gold makes the golden rules. So if you ain't making no money and you're reading this book and somebody else is paying the bills, skip this part. As a matter of fact, cut it out and give it to them.)

Rule number one: When you come home, there will be no loud music playing what you don't want to hear. It has to go off.

Rule number two: If you have maids in your house — and everybody who has children has maids (I explained this earlier on, but it bears repeating), make sure your children have chores and responsibilities to keep the house clean. That's the great thing about having kids. You don't have to clean up no more — or cook — as soon as they get to an age where they're able to do that.

Rule number three: Refer to rules number one and two.

If those rules don't work, here's my solution to achieve quick stress reduction: I pull out my pistol. If you're lucky, you may only need to do it one time, because after that they'll know you mean business. If somebody's screaming and yelling after I've had a hard day at work, all I need to do is just tap my purse. If I go into my closet and reach up high, everybody in my house gets real quiet, because they know where I'm going.

Again, I repeat: you have to have some mechanism to keep them quiet. Some people use the Bible. Some people use reverse psychology. I ain't got time for all of that. So I pull my piece out of my purse to get some peace. I make peace with a piece of steel.

If you'd rather not use a gun, here's another method I've found very effective. As I mentioned earlier on, if you're training a puppy not to pee on your carpet, you make him smell it and tap him with some newspaper two or three times. That puppy will never pee on your carpet again. It's the same thing with getting peace in your house. Let me explain in detail.

If you go crazy one good time and lose your mind and start breaking everybody's stuff but your own, the next time they start to work on your nerves, all you have to do is walk toward anything that's breakable. They will become very quiet. I like that sort of psychology — I think it's called "behavior modification." Teach them — puppies, husbands, men, women, children, whatever — these rules will work. All you got to do is do it one time — it's a deterrent. From then on, everybody knows, "Well, you know, my momma is crazy as hell — maybe I need to sit down." "Sit down." "Shut up." "Get out of the way." You might need to spend a couple of nights in jail, but they'll know to shut the hell up.

MOTHER'S SAYINGS OF WISDOM

Always wear clean drawers, my momma used to say, 'cause if you get hit by a car and you've got on dirty drawers, I ain't coming down to see you in the hospital. You ain't going to be embarrassing me." But then I thought, if you get hit by a car and it hits you in the right place, don't you mess up your drawers anyway? So that didn't make sense.

But she had this thing, "Every good-bye ain't gone and every shut-eye ain't asleep." This meant that you always have to pay attention to people. You don't let them fool you. Because if you think they're gone, they might still be there. So watch what you say. If you think they're asleep, be careful, because they might be awake, watching everything you're doing.

SAYING YES WHEN YOU MEAN NO

Trying to please everybody else — you're never in your life going to be happy. You know, I learned a long time ago . . . a lady told me before she died . . . it was the simplest thing. . . . "Only say what you can do." When she told me that, it stuck with me all my life. I don't sit there and lie to nobody, telling them I'm going to do something when I know I ain't going to do it.

I ain't going to sit there and tell you yes when I mean no. I'm going to tell you no. If you keep telling people no and they keep trying to change your mind, what the hell is that? They're trying to control you. I don't understand that. "You're trying to control me — I done told you no, so get the hell out of here. Don't sit there and ask me the same thing over and over and over again."

If people learn to stand up and say no, they'll be a lot happier. You can't please everybody. If you set out to please everybody, you're going to be the one who's miserable. These folks in this world are something else.

DREAMS

I dream from time to time about numbers. You know, if you dream about fish, it means somebody in your family's pregnant. I ain't had one of those dreams in a long time. If you dream about fish and monkeys and sharks, that means they're pregnant with an ugly baby. That's what they say back in Louisiana. Every now and then, I have a nightmare. My last nightmare, I was wrestling with a bear. . . . Oh, no, that was Cora's daddy, I'm sorry.

A Little Bit of Suffering
Is a Good Thing

Being poor and broke and having to figure things out, that's why you don't see a whole bunch of black folks committing suicide. Hell, we have been through the worst of it, broke and poor. We know how to make it poor. Like if we got a whole bunch of money and went broke again, hell, we've done it. With the stock market crash, folks who ain't never been broke were jumping out of windows and all that foolishness. We ain't going to do that.

I feel sorry for these kids that have everything handed to them. I look at these little white kids, that Paris Hilton and all those other little kids that have everything. They ain't never had to suffer or struggle a day in their lives. That's tough. I'm glad my child suffered and understood what it was like to have it rough. So when you get to the other side, you can appreciate it.

Hell, we know how to make it on a can of tuna and pork and beans for two weeks. Suffering and hardship are a good thing, because they build character. You want to have a good character. You want to have richness in your life. The suffering and the struggling till the soil to get ready for good things to grow up out of it.

When It's Okay to
Give Someone Advice

We talked about this earlier on in the chapter about getting young people to wake up. I may be repeating myself a little bit, but the time you spend reading this will save you a whole bunch of wasted time giving people advice that they don't want to hear, let alone use.

First of all, before I open my mouth, I'm going to look at the person that you are, what you do, how you do, how you think, how you act. Then I'm going to pick your brain a little bit before you sit there and ask me for advice. I had this friend named Nikki. I used to give Nikki advice all of the time. Give Nikki advice . . . Nikki . . . Nikki . . . Nikki. It would go in one ear — she'd sit there and listen to it — and come right out the other. She would never put it into action.

I stop giving advice when I'm telling folks the same thing over and over and over again, and they ain't getting better, they ain't changing. Don't come over here asking me what you need to do and you ain't going to do it. I hate wasting my time talking to folks about what they need to do. I know what I need to do, and if I figure it out, I do it. I'm a person who likes to take action.

Don't waste my time if you ain't going to do it. So if you take the advice and you put it into action, then you are somebody I want to talk to. That's how I'm going to challenge you. I'm going to give you a little bit of advice first and see what you do with it. If you do the right thing with it, then I'll give you some more.

I ain't going sit there wasting two or three days trying to talk you into getting better when you don't want to be. Some folks don't want to be better. Some folks *say* they want to be better, but all they want to do is stay at the same spot all their lives.

As long as you don't have information, you ain't responsible for it. The minute you get the information on what you need to do, you're responsible for it. If you don't do it, you're going to stay right where you're at.

WHEN IS IT GOSSIP AND WHEN IS IT JUST USEFUL INFORMATION?

If a little gossip can save lives, then I'm all for it. See, there was some gossip that this woman had HIV. I wanted to go tell the man, "Now, the rumor's going around. You be careful what you're doing." If you're friends with the woman, she's going to be mad. I say the hell with it. She's just going to have to be mad. I walked up to the both of them and said, "There's a rumor going around, and you all need to sit down and talk about that if it's the path you're going to go on." Both of them are mad at me. They don't speak to me. But that was gossip that turned out to be useful information.

Otherwise, I don't believe in gossip. I don't like sitting around talking about nobody. I can't stand all those tabloids because you never know what's true and what's not. And I don't give a damn if J.Lo's got a ring on her. None of that matters. That's stupid. That's not going to add one string of hair to your head or another good day on this earth to you. But a lot of folks get into all that because they don't have nothing else to do in their lives. Hell, I've got enough drama in my own life. I don't need to go sitting around peeking at nobody else. I live in the ghetto. I've got to walk two blocks to get to the store and try not to get shot. I've got enough excitement. I don't have to jump out of no plane, do no bungee jumping. All I got to do is walk to the store. That's all the excitement I need.

MY WORST FEAR

Michael Jackson.

No, my worst fear is when you've got people around you that you love, your fear becomes something happening to any of them. Like Cora, my sister, a nephew, a niece that you worry about. But that's about it. The worst that can happen has already happened to me. Hell, I've been broke. Couldn't eat. Struggling. I've been through all of that. I ain't even scared of jail. That used to be my worst fear.

If I get afraid of something or anxious, I've got to confront it, go and figure out what that is. What the Bible say, be anxious for nothing. Whatever is making you feel anxious and nervous, go deal with it. Sure, it will get you down for a minute. You sit there in the room, dark and depressed and all that other stuff. Open the curtains. Get up and do something. Confront it. You can't live your life that way. There's so much hell going on in the world right now, every day that you wake up is a gift. So you need to take that for what it's worth and enjoy. A lot of the worst things that can happen to you, you don't really have too much control over, so confront what you can.

LIFE IS NOT FAIR

I believe that. Everybody is dealt a different hand, but you have to do what you have with your hand. If your hand is terrible, you got to play it. I don't think it's an excuse. Life is not fair. But we don't ever want life to be fair, because if we start getting the things that we deserve, none of us would be here. I'm glad life is not fair.

You know, I sit there and look . . . I've been around a lot of folks, some of the poorest black people in the world, in the ghetto and projects . . . but laughing, joking, having a good time, enjoying their life every day. And I've seen some of the richest folks just sitting around uptight, like a stick up their butt, just can't move, everything is so posh . . . it just blows my mind. They've got everything in the world, and they're sitting there and they ain't happy? But I remember back in the day when we were poor we were having a good time with nothing. So, even though you might have a whole bunch of stuff, that don't necessarily make it fair. Life is what you make of it. You take your hand. You take your pot. And you make you a good old soup and go with it.

I think we have the power to change. You don't have any choice of who you're born to or where you come from. But you do have a choice of where you go from there. I think that we have the power, each and every one of us, every day, to change our lives.

COMMON SENSE

I'm going to save the printer's ink on this one. This is the shortest chapter in this book because common sense is summed up in three words: keep it simple.

You know, people don't want their intelligence insulted. They don't want to be preached to. They don't want to be degraded. All they want to do is sit, laugh, have a good time, love one another, forget about what's going on in the world, and find something out so they can be useful in this life. Do this and you have common sense.

IT'S NOT HOW YOU PLAY THE GAME, BUT IF YOU WIN

For me, it's all about winning. You know, I've gotten a little older now, so I understand that sometimes you win and sometimes you lose. But it's how you play the game, like people say. To hell with all of that, I'm going to win! It's losers who say that kind of stuff! "Well, well, we're all winners in the end" — that's a loser talking.

I like to win. I play cards every Saturday night. We make money on those card games — and I win. I won't tell this in print, but I cheat . . . to win.

My secret tricks? You see, I'm full figure, so

I've got more layers and secret hiding places on my body than most people have. I do more before 5 A.M. than most people do all day — trying to wash this body, so I know where every crack and crevice is. I can just sit there at the table and slide a card up any one of these rolls, and they don't know it's there.

I don't count cards. Hell no. You know how much glaucoma medicine I'd have to smoke to be able to count all those cards? I just have another set in my pocket. Not a real pocket in my dress, but these pockets of fat.

I've been caught. But the first thing you do when you get caught is jump up and act like you're crazy as hell. "You better leave me alone! Get the hell out of my face." It works. People leave you alone. "I ain't cheating, you bastard!" Just start cussing, they usually leave you alone. But they know you're crazy. I've shot a few folks — I never admitted I was cheating.

I know you're going to ask the question. No, the cards don't fall out when I jump up and down. The deeper you put it up under there . . . see, what you need to understand is I got a rib cage up under here somewhere. So you put the cards closer up under your rib cage and act like you're scratching to get it out. Also, at this age, I don't jump up and

232

down so high. I don't get past three or four inches off the ground — or let a man tell it, twelve inches off the ground — but it's only about three or four inches.

■ ■ ■ ■

PART ELEVEN
MADEA CUTS TO THE CHASE

■ ■ ■ ■

GETTING ANGRY

I am able to be reasonable with you up to a point. But Lord help you if you're sitting there being nasty to me or talking to me any kind of way. That's why I don't understand women who'd let a man talk to them in an abusive way. Abuse is abuse from all sides of it. If he's hitting you, it's one thing. If he's talking to you like a dog, it's the same thing. You don't let people mistreat and mishandle you.

When someone is demeaning me and doing all sorts of crazy stuff, that's when it's time to get mad. I'll take it up to a certain point. A lot of times what happens when people see you get mad (especially if it's your first time getting mad with them), they will change their attitude. They might say, "Well, I've been doing this so long, why are you getting mad all of a sudden?" However, they will start changing the way they treat you if you're dealing with somebody with a little sense. If they're crazy, it ain't going to matter. They're going to keep treating you the way they've been treating you.

My anger, for me — I'm extreme — I don't go zero-one-two-three to ten. I go zero to fifty. So I'm going to sit there and try to talk it out with you for a few seconds. If you're still going to be nasty, watch out, because there ain't no medium — it's hold on tight, I'm going straight to hot! I'm going to warm it up in the room. Listen, I don't just get up and leave the room, unless the place is torn up. By then, it's time to go anyway, because the police is on the way. When you hear sirens in the distance, then it's time to leave.

"Take your earrings off!" That is the black woman's national anthem. She's getting ready to fight. Anybody who knows that (even if you ain't black), if you see a black woman doing that, get ready. I'll be in my room, taking off my earrings, just getting ready to go to bed. Right then, my husband used to jump up and stand in the corner, because he didn't know what was going on.

Men, please fold over the top of this page so you can quickly refer to this lifesaving information. Watch for this first signal of danger. If she begins to take off the first earring, you need to jump in quickly to defuse the situation, right away. That is the key to stopping all hell from breaking loose. If you can keep the black woman's earrings on, you might have a chance at getting away without being hurt. If one of them comes off, that's about a fifty percent chance of an asswhupping. If they both come off, she's going to jail. If the woman even touches her earring, it's a sign to calm her the hell down! If you think she's scratching her earlobe, that's a red flag — that's 9-1-1 to the brain that we're getting ready to go into overdrive.

HOLDING ON TO HATRED AND ANGER

Anger is a good thing. If you're angry, that's fine. Be angry. Get it out, because anger is like fire. It will purge and cleanse. Just don't get bitter about it. Bitterness is like cancer. I believe that people will be so mad with folks for years and years and years — and people are dead and gone, they're still mad at them. What will happen is that bitterness will sit down in you and become a cancer. I believe when you put those kinds of things in your body, they become real stuff, like sickness and disease. Your body's holding on to it, so it has to manifest in some sort of way. That's what I really believe.

You can't hold on to things. I will punch

people in the face and fight to keep from getting bitter. See, I like to get even every now and again. If I have to walk up and do what I need to do to be all right with you, you need to let me do that. If I've got to cuss you out one good time, that's fine.

I'm not mad at Brown. Brown's all right. I was madder at me for that night. Remember what I said earlier, if you've got one finger pointing at someone, you've got the rest of them pointing back at you. You've got to remember some of the things you've done. That person that you're mad at may not be on the same level in life where you're at. Everything that's happened to you can work for the good if you let it.

Clean it up, and please don't dump it onto your children. Why is it that we just take our bottled-up anger and pass it on to our offspring? The thing I can't stand is when a grown-up who's frustrated and angry with their own life tells a child that he or she ain't going to be nothing! It's bad enough that so many kids face things that want to keep them from being what they can be in the world without a parent doing that.

Parents (and this goes for teachers and anybody else who cares for children), you never know who you're raising. Look at the life experiences of people like Oprah and others like her who had a whole bunch of stuff trying to destroy them — and see what they have become now. You never know who that child is going to be.

BREAKING UP FIGHTS

I'll say something to children. But not these days — back in the day, all you had to do is walk up and they'd break up. But now these children are shooting and acting crazy. Back in the day, all they had were knives, and you could deal with that. Now they got Uzis and machine guns. I ain't Wonder Woman. I can't block those bullets. But if they're older, I will try to get into it, because they know better. But it's going to take a miracle to get these young kids raised. It's going to take parents getting back to being parents, like daddies staying home and acting like men and taking care of their children. Mommas are doing what they can. It's hard for a woman to raise a boy child.

You've got to be able to assess the situation. See, there are certain kinds of fighters and there are certain kinds of shooters. If you're in a situation where you know this thing's going to escalate, then get the hell out of the way. Say what you're going to say to them and get into the middle of it. But if you see it's getting out of control, then get the hell out of there. Each situation calls for a separate response.

SPEAKING TO STUPID PEOPLE WHO LOOK DOWN ON YOU

Those people who think they're better than you, who patronize and speak down on you, a lot of those people aren't worth the bother. You see, I get mad and I want to fight, and I'm going to prove to them that I'm not as ignorant as they think I am. You see, what they'll do is they'll provoke you by saying stupid stuff to you and making you think that you're less than they are. Then, when you start acting less and start kicking some ass, then they get mad. So that's a no-win situation. What I try to do is avoid them at all costs. I see them coming.

But if you have to talk to them, here's what you do. First, you try to start off as intelligent as possible. These are the rules. Number one: if they say something that's condescending, you start off as intelligent as you possibly can. Whatever they say, you say, "Well, I don't think that's correct," and "Please refrain from speaking to me in that manner again." If they continue, then you start with one little word that they can understand that may be a little profane: "If you don't leave me the hell alone, I'm going to lose all my dignity and beat the hell out of you." If they still continue, then you provide an ass-whupping as promised.

WHEN VIOLENCE IS NECESSARY

I like to be able to get results — and sometimes getting results means redecorating the room — turning over the furniture, putting holes in the wall. That way, everybody comes running, trying to see what's happening. And, believe it or not, I feel better after it's done, because whatever I'm frustrated about, once I get through tearing up the place, I feel relieved.

Oh, well, as long as it ain't my place. You always got to remember — when you get mad, don't tear up nothing in your own house. You ain't never that mad. If it's your man's house, you can tear it up — or the restaurant, you can tear it up, but don't tear up your own place — because then, you're going be mad after you get mad, because you done tore up your place. If you damage the restaurant, they're probably going to go after you with the bill. But again, I write checks and hope to make it to the bank.

WHEN IT'S OKAY TO HAVE A PISTOL

I got my first gun when I started stripping. My momma always had guns. We knew not to touch them because she'd shoot you if you did. We just knew better back then. When I told her I was stripping, she said, "You're going to need this for protection." She was right, for I sure needed it more than a couple of times. People don't know how to keep their hands off you. They think after you leave work that you're supposed to go home with them — and I wasn't no ho. I was a stripper. There's a difference! I was a classy stripper!

My first gun was a little .22 that would fit right under my breasts. I'd be up there stripping and nobody would ever see it. I could lift one breast up and put it right under it all night long and just pull it out when I needed it. I was a quick draw unless I was sweaty, because everything would get slippery. Women don't sweat — they glisten. No hell, I sweat like a football player, like a linebacker. I didn't use any baby oil or Vaseline when I was out there. I'd just go out there and shake two times and I'd be sweating.

My momma didn't give me any instruction on the gun. She just told me, "Aim and pull." That was it. "Hit your target. If you miss it, keep shooting — eventually you'll hit something." She didn't bother cleaning them. If it got dirty, backfiring and jammed up with gunpowder, she'd just throw it away and steal another one. She never used the guns on the children. All she needed for us was the bag of belts.

My old .22 was passed down to me, but I've upgraded, since that one, one that was from my momma's momma. They always kept these pistols around because you never knew when somebody was going to get out of line. If my daddy came in fussing and drunk, my momma would just lay the pistol on the table and go to bed, he'd just shut up. It's a peacemaker. You see, the Bible says, peace be still. But peace is made of steel. If you have some steel, you can keep some peace. That's what I believe.

The history is that if no man was around, you had to protect yourself and your children from the KKK. Before you had the boys *with* the hoods, now you got to be worrying about the boys *in* the 'hood!

If they come knocking on the door in the middle of the night trying to rob you, you got to have something to protect yourself. When you get older — that's another good excuse why you need protection from these folks. I like somebody trying to take advantage of me because I'm old and weak. Then I have to prove to them that I might look old, but don't let that gray hair fool you. Ain't nobody going to come snatching my purse without me lightening up that ass. It's going to be crazy. We're going to have some fun. I like all that foolishness, that drama.

The neighborhood has changed. A lot of people who owned their own homes died, and now the houses are being rented out by a bunch of fools. They know I ain't got no bars on my window. I ain't got no security alarm. I can leave that house for weeks and weeks and come back there and everything is fine. Hey, I can go up there and sleep and you could push slightly the front door and walk right in. Most of the time, I don't even lock it. Because they know if they come upstairs messing with me, my nine million friends are going to be in there waiting for them — that's my 9-millimeter.

Every now and then, we'll get somebody new that's moved onto the block and think they can play the music as loud as they want. I have to go knock on the door and say — and I'm really nice — "This is a nice neighborhood, we don't have all of that, can you turn the music down?" That's the way it starts, and they'll turn it down, they'll apologize and do the right thing. Most of them have sense. But, you know, one of them told me to go to hell. They had to call the police because I set it off. I went up in the house and tore the stereo up and broke all the records and CDs and other stuff. Then he told the police, "This old lady's crazy, this old lady's crazy!"

"No," I said. "I told them to turn it down." The next time, those boys driving by with those boom boxes in their cars will turn them down when they get to my block. Once they drive by my house, they turn it back up again.

I set the boundaries in my neighborhood, and I think it takes the neighborhood to set the boundaries. If everybody in the neighborhood comes together to say what they're not going to tolerate, you can really clean things up. It's almost like one of those homeowner associations. Even though we're in the 'hood, we can still get organized. We ain't going to have no dope dealers hanging out on the corners selling dope. We ain't going to have any of this because we're going to run this neighborhood. If they don't like it, they're going to get the hell out of it.

GETTING RESPECT IN OLD AGE

People in their thirties and forties look at me as if they think I have something to say or give. The young folk just think I'm funny. They think I'm a joke. I can sit around making them laugh. I'd like to play basketball with them, but I can't anymore. You know, my breasts are heavy and they're hurting when I'm jumping up and down like that. I can't do that anymore.

But what I figured out what to do is that if you want to reach them — you make them laugh and then you can give them some of that same wisdom. See, grown folk come to you to get it because they know you got it and they know you know what to do with it. But the children think you're out there joking, laughing, and listening to their kind of music and you're hanging right there with them and having a good time. Then, before they even know it, you've left some wisdom in them that they can use.

So I make them laugh. It's not to say that one of them little badasses will come there and make me mad. All I have to do is hem one of them up and the rest of them respect me. See, that's what happens. One of them talked a little crazy with me, and I went out there and popped him upside the head. He went home crying to his momma. Now, when they talk, they say, "Hey, how you doing?" Again, we call this Madea's science of behavior modification!

MADEA'S LAST WORD

If somebody asked me what's the best advice you have to give, get ready. You may forget everything else I've told you, but I hope this sticks in your heart. One thing you learn at my age is that we ain't got time to waste. The biggest waste is that we spend so much time being worried and crazy about things that really don't matter in the long run. So maybe this will help you figure things out a little better. Here it goes:

Some people come into your life for a lifetime and some come for a season. You have to know which is which. I put everybody that comes into my life in the category of a tree. Some people are leaves on a tree. The wind blows, they go to the left. The wind blows from the other way, they go to the right. They are just unstable. You can't count on them for nothing. All they ever do is take from that tree. What you need to understand about a leaf is that it has a season. It'll wither and die and blow away. There ain't no need to be praying over a leaf to be resurrected. When it's dead it's gone. Let it go. Some people are like that. All the leaf ever does is cool you off every now and then. If you're grown, you know what I'm talking about, because you can call them in the middle of the night and get cooled off. That's the leaf people. They come to take.

Then there are people like a branch. You got to be careful with branch people. They come in all different shapes and sizes. You never know how strong they will be in your life. So my advice is to tip out on it slowly. When you're going out on a limb, don't put too much weight on it at once, because it can fall and leave you high and dry. Sometimes, you have to wait for a branch to grow up before it can hold all of the things you want to share with it.

Finally, there are people who are like the roots at the bottom of the tree. If you find yourself two or three people in your entire lifetime that are like the roots, then you are blessed. The roots don't care nothing about being seen. All they're there to do is hold that tree up, to make sure it stays in the air. It comes from the earth to give that tree everything it needs. That's what relationships should be about. That's what you need, people who want to be in your life for the right reasons.

If somebody wants to walk out of your life, you've got to LET THEM GO. When you learn to love yourself, you will end up giving standards to everybody around you. Again, I repeat for emphasis, if they don't meet those standards, you have to let them go, because they might be a leaf. And forgive them with all your might.

So, I'm glad that you've read my first book

and that you made it to the end of it. I hope it helps you as you walk around day to day, and you think about the things said in this book. We Madeas may not be around like we used to, but I hope that I've left enough behind of our stories and our wisdom to help you. So if you need anything as you go through life, keep a few copies of this book around to refer back to from time to time.

EPILOGUE

by Tyler Perry

Do you know it's awesome to have people come up to me and say, "Thanks for telling my story. . . . Thanks for letting me see me. . . . Thanks for letting me know what I needed to do for this situation." It is an experience that is surreal and overwhelming. But it also lets me know that I am where I'm supposed to be in this life. I give praise to God every day for it. What rings true is that everything we go through in life will work for our good. One day I realized that all the things that I have endured were for the benefit of helping potentially millions of other people, helping us to laugh through this life. That is the amazing and powerful gift from which I draw strength to go on to the next thing.

Laughter is the anesthetic I use to get to everything else. A lot of what I do in the show is about showing reflections to help and encourage people.

What I love about Madea is that she has a heart of gold. She tough. She's got this incredible exterior. That's why people love her. They know her. She takes no crap. Madea is the kind of person who will beat the hell out of you one minute and take you to the doctor the next — to make sure you're okay. Overall, the people who know her — those of us who remember this kind of character from back in the day — know that she's got the best heart in the world. She's no fool, but she'll give you every dime that she has to make sure you're okay.

Remember, you have to forgive so that you can be forgiven. And sometimes, you have to do that with all your might.

Yes, Madea might not be on every corner anymore. Maybe the government should put her on the endangered species list. The laughter and enjoyment that she generates give me hope that her spirit is alive and well and will continue to burn in every one of us as we journey though this remarkable life.

Now that you're finished with this book, I hope that you have laughed, that you're lighter than when you started. If it were a great steak, I'd tell you to eat the meat and leave the bone. If there was something here that was jarring or that you didn't find humorous, I'd love you to look closer at

Madea. If you don't know Madea, I'd advise you to take a look at some of her DVDs and films. You'll see that even though she's sometimes a little rough around the edges, she has a lot of love and wisdom to share.

In addition to making you laugh, I hope there is something that she has said that has inspired you and even awakened something in your spirit to motivate you to become an even better human being.

ABOUT THE AUTHOR

Madea, whose real name is Mabel Simmons, was born — according to most accounts — in rural Greensburg, Louisiana, in 1937. (Other accounts show her as older; some have speculated the discrepancy might have been related to attempts to qualify earlier for Social Security benefits.) Already a star of stage and screen, she is ready to take the world of books by storm.

Tyler Perry is a playwright, director, producer, composer, and actor. He is the creative and entrepreneurial force behind ten blockbuster theatrical productions that have had sold-out national tours. He is also the writer, producer, and star of the hit movies *Diary of a Mad Black Woman* and *Madea's Family Reunion* (which he also directed). *Don't Make a Black Woman Take Off Her Earrings* is his first book. He lives in Atlanta.